The Designated Motivator: Unlock Your Secret Superpower to Change Your Life, the World and Everyone In It

Inspired by the Eastern Connecticut State University Lady Warrior Softball Team 2019

Dawn W. Brolin, CPA, CFE

THE DESIGNATED MOTIVATOR

The Designated Motivator - An individual who has the passion and ability to give others the greatest gift of all: the realization and mobilization of their true potential. Someone who uses a specific mindset and skill set to empower others to believe in themselves so they can achieve at higher levels than they thought were possible.

Contents

FOREWORD

Mike Michalowicz

Designated Motivator for Entrepreneurs

Folks come from all over the globe to attend our annual ProfitCON event. The hundreds of people are from different countries and different backgrounds. Some are accountants and some are bookkeepers. Others are business coaches. And still others are entrepreneurs of different vocations. All are looking to bring their business to the next level.

The event happens over four days and the last day of presentations ends with a strong keynote performance. I liken it to the finale of a fireworks display: people expect it to be spectacular. Last year, Dawn Brolin was the closing keynote. She was the year prior, too. And the year prior to that. Yes, she is that good.

Dawn is the Designated Motivator (DM) for our event. She brings an unmatched energy level and powerful simplicity to her presentations. She delivers insights that can not only be absorbed, but can be done. She gets the audience believing in themselves.

Every good conference needs a DM, and so does every good organization.

I have seen struggling teams become elite performers, by having a Designated Motivator. I have seen humdrum meetings move to high energy, results driving huddles, by having a DM. And I have seen our own business outpace our competition day in and day out, year after year, because of our DM. You and your company are about to experience the same.

As you start to read this book, you will feel the energy yourself. You will feel a shift inside you that can never be undone. You will find that there is a Designated Motivator waiting to be awakened in you and anyone you, well, designate.

When you become a DM it exponentially improves every area of your life. Your business will improve, your personal life will improve, the people in your orbit will be more engaged. You will thrive. The people who benefit from the DM will also have improvement throughout their lives.

Now don't worry! As you embrace your Designated Motivator, you will not lose who you are. You won't need to become someone else. You don't need to become a Tony Robbins or one of those hyper infomercial guys. You will simply be more of who you already are. With the tools in this book, you will be able to harness the power of your natural self and amplify the performance of everyone around you (including yourself.)

As a DM you will help define the highest purpose of your organization and align the entire team around it. The purpose won't be "to achieve more shareholder profits" or "to provide proficient service," although those will be natural outcomes. Your purpose will be something that resonates throughout the organization and motivates everyone.

As a DM you will increase the happiness, joy and positive energy of your organization and yourself. It won't be through inauthentic "I'm good enough, I'm smart enough, and gosh darn it, people like me, " Stuart Smalley affirmations. Instead, you will leverage the DM tools that bring natural happiness and positive energy, authentically.

As a DM you will experience great productivity and output from your work team and others in your community. You will not need to "whip people into shape" or "micro-manage employees." Instead, you will channel the long lasting effects of self-motivation and aspiration that DMs bring out of the people around them (including themselves).

And as a DM, you will create transformational, life-altering experiences for yourself and others.

I suspect, in your life, you may have already crossed paths with DMs without realizing it. That best teacher you had, who connected with you in a deeper way, is a DM. That family member who understands you and energizes you is a DM. That stranger who said the right thing in the right way at the right time is a DM. Those people are all DMs, albeit in flash moments, in your life. Now as a DM yourself, you will deliberately and regularly bring similar experiences to others. Their lives will forever be changed, and forever better, as a result.

I suspect you may be excited to dig in right now, but may also feel skeptical. After all, this does sound a bit like a love child of Tony Robbins and Stuart Smalley. But I assure you, it's not. I know this because I have experienced it and lived it. Dawn has guided me to be the DM in my business, in my family and in countless aspects of my life. It has been transformative for me.

My business is performing at its highest levels ever. My family is engaged and supportive of each other like never before. And life is simply better. Yours is about to be, too.

My DM Dedication

"What you do makes a difference, and you have to decide what kind of difference you want to make." — Jane Goodall

I decided a long time ago that I wanted to make a difference--that is how I started down this DM path. I felt the desire in my soul and the fire in my belly to do what I could to make people realize how gifted they are and to help them see and seize the possibility they had within them.

This book was inspired by each of those people who have come into my life. Those special, unique and amazing individuals. All of whom have taught me something--and who have helped me become a better version of myself. One that I hope continues to make a positive impact in the world in new and meaningful ways.

While my career, coaching and other commitments may have taken me physically away from home over the years, the inspiration for this book-- and all that I do-- remains my family. Kevin, Emily and Kayla, you mean the world to me and in my heart you will always be my #1 people and priority. Thank you for all of the joy, beautiful memories and motivation you provide on a daily basis. I love you all more than words can say.

This book was also inspired by the 2019 Lady Warriors team at Eastern Connecticut State University. Wow! What an amazing experience we had ladies! It has been a privilege and an honor to get to know each of you and to watch you grow as individuals and a team. I thank you for allowing me to be your DM in so many wild and crazy ways. I know that all of you will accomplish amazing things as you continue to forge your paths toward your highest potential.

As we walk through life, there are some people who we will know for only a short period, and some who will choose to stay with us for the long haul (Thank you, Kevin Brolin!). The people who I have had the opportunity to know deeply have my gratitude and thanks. Whether you know it or not, our interactions have helped me see my own gifts and potential, while I hope I have done the same for you in return.

There is nothing that makes my spirit and heart soar more than to see someone rise to realize their greatness. If I can play a part in helping them do that, then I believe it is my duty to assist them in whatever way I can as a DM. I encourage you to use your DM superpower to do the same.

For those DMs who have helped me to achieve my goals and become the person I am today, please accept my sincerest gratitude. You have all made a profound difference and I promise to pay it forward.

As a final note of thanks here, I would also like to acknowledge author, speaker and all-around Designated Motivator for businesses Mike Michalowicz for writing the foreword to this book and for his profound inspiration for business owners like me. I appreciate your support and all of your amazing gifts more than you could ever know, Mike! Check him out at mikemichalowicz.com

I would also like to thank Gaynor Hardy Meilke who was instrumental in helping to bring this book and the DM philosophy into the world-- without her, this book would still be just a collection of thoughts in my brain!

Wishing you success and happiness,

Dawn Brolin

This Secret Will Change Your Life—
But You Must Act Now!

I want to give you the goods up front. I'm a CPA by profession, so I get the numbers: I have about 10 seconds to capture your attention and pique your curiosity enough for you to invest any more of your precious time in reading this book.

The good news is, I only need a moment to let you in on the secret you will learn in this book:

You possess a superpower that can save lives and have a profound, positive impact on the world.

Now that you know the secret, you have an important choice to make:

Act now, and learn how to use it at full force, or let it die with you.

I hope you choose to act. Even if you don't read the rest of this book to learn how to mobilize this secret for your own greater good and that of the people around you, it is my greatest wish that in this brief moment that we have connected, you realize the potential and power you have to do amazing things. All you need is someone like me, a Designated Motivator (DM for short), to help you see and seize it.

We all have a limited amount of time on this earth and I want you to use your inner DM to better your own life and to benefit everyone who crosses your path: So don't wait—take ACTION—use your experiences and passion to tap into the secret superpower that we all possess but few of us unleash at its full force: the Designated Motivator.

The Designated Motivator Mindset: Your Secret Sauce for Success

In my experience, harnessing your DM can exponentially improve every area of your universe and those of the people in your orbit. For example it can:

- Help you define and act in alignment with your highest purpose.
- Increase your internal happiness and positive external energy.
- Improve relationships with your family, friends and colleagues.
- Allow you to achieve greater productivity and teamwork at work and in other organizations you are involved in.
- Help you create transformative, life-altering experiences for yourself and others.

Perhaps this sounds like some pie-in-the-sky self-motivational guru talk. It's not. I know this because I have seen the power of being a Designated Motivator for others and experiencing the impact of having a DM in my own life. That's the wonderful and awesome thing about The Designated Motivator Philosophy. It's a two-way street—you can give and you can receive. It's all up to you.

Before we go any further, let me define exactly what I mean when I say DM (we're going to refer to it as DM after this point for easy reference) so we are on the same page:

The Designated Motivator - An individual who has the passion and ability to give others the greatest gift of all: the realization and mobilization of their true potential. Someone who uses a specific mindset and skill set to empower others to believe in themselves so they can achieve at higher levels than they thought were possible.

4

Does this sound like you? Or someone you might know? Maybe you are still a little skeptical about the power and impact of this idea. That's good. It's important that you don't just take my word for it.

I want you to really feel and experience the benefits of the DM Philosophy, Mindset and Skill Set for yourself. You can choose to read about how I discovered my own DM abilities and then use the DM Toolkit I have included to apply the principles to your own life. If you prefer just to jump to the tools, that's cool too. The important thing is to take action now toward your own goals as a DM.

However you consume this DM book, it's pretty much guaranteed that if you apply the concept regularly, you will have a profoundly positive and truly transformative impact on the people and organizations who need your gift as a DM most.

My Secret Revealed

*"I want to inspire people. I want someone to look at me
and say, 'Because of you I didn't give up.'"* — Unknown

The discovery of a secret is a funny thing. Usually the secret isn't a secret, rather, it is actually something that is already a "thing" until you experience it. I believe that at some point in your life you have an experience that is either positive or negative and finally, you "get it." "You are able to identify with a particular experience and it turns into part of who you are, who people see you as, and when it's a positive experience, it changes the way you live your life for the better.

For me, this secret—more like a revelation—was that I discovered I had the ability to be a motivator. I always thought of myself as a positive person, someone who gives 110% to others. I regularly put myself aside to ensure that other people were taken care of and lifted up. I didn't think this was anything special, since so many people have this gift and practice and pass on positivity every day. What I came to realize, however, was this motivation thing is a whole other animal—and it requires a very specific shift in your mindset and skill set.

Let me explain:

The ability to make another human being smile, laugh and feel good about themselves and their accomplishments, doesn't necessarily result in a successful moment. This behavior and these characteristics are what I would define as being an encourager. Being a *motivator* is a much different and a much more powerful gift.

A motivator is someone who not only makes people feel good, but also has the ability to spark positive action in themselves and others. This spark fuels an individual or a group of individuals to accomplish things they never imagined were possible.

If you feel the urge and passion to help others realize their own gifts and true potential then you have the power to be what I call a Designated Motivator. The person who gives others the greatest gift of all--the ability to believe in themselves and to tap into their true potential to achieve at higher levels than they thought possible.

Again, this may sound like some "motivational guru" jargon...it is not. Most people never achieve their own greatness because they either don't recognize it, or don't know how to empower it in the world. As I mentioned previously, I cannot imagine a more powerful or purposeful role than that of the DM.

It was this secret that I uncovered about myself that helped me step into my DM role fully and to live each day out loud (Yep, I am that person you can hear across the room when I get going, which is pretty much all the time!). I use my voice to celebrate others and lift them up as much as I can. I feel this is what I was born to do, and I have had others' say the same thing. But I don't want you to take my words for it. I want to hear it from the people whom I have taken on a DM role directly, that's why I included some of their perspectives throughout the book.

These thoughts are shared from family, clients, teammates and players not to show my greatness in any way...I just think their words are the most powerful way for you to understand how becoming a DM can truly transform others. I want to give you some concrete examples to inspire you to do the same. In your own DM style, of course!

To begin this journey that we are undertaking, let's start with my dear friend, Morgan Perry, and her take on the power of a DM in her own life.

The Lifelong Impact Created by a Designated Motivator

Morgan Perry

"To me, a Designated Motivator is a champion who won't let you give up."

Dawn was my high school basketball coach. She was like no one I had ever met and that's still the case.

We both attended Parrish Hill High School in the same small town. She was barely out of college and she came back to coach our team. She was beyond driven to help us get better and to be winners—on and off the court.

Dawn made it clear from the beginning that she believed in me, and she was the one person who made me start thinking about bigger dreams for myself.

At that time, I didn't see my own potential, but Dawn did. She built me up and made me believe that I could play at college. "Where there's a will there's a way," she always told me.

What was truly amazing to me about Dawn is that she knew what she wanted and she made the things she wanted come to life. It was an intangible quality at first in my mind, but it transformed into a tangible result. For Dawn, not doing what she set out to do wasn't an option.

She really taught me about the importance of using the power of one's thoughts to create the life you want.

For example, Dawn's name was on the banner in the high school gym as the highest-scoring female and during my junior year I surpassed her record while she was coaching me. It was a big moment to earn a spot on that banner. I still hold the record of highest scorer in the history of the school, for both boys and girls.

Through Dawn's ability to motivate and coach me, I became the first student to earn a Division I scholarship from our school. She really took me under her wing. She knew I needed someone to encourage me and build me up.

In my last year of college, our team went to the NCAA Division III Championship. It was a huge deal and Dawn visited with me before we went. I had transferred in my senior year of college from Division I to Division III and helped the team make it to the NCAA Division III championship. I believe it was Dawn's belief in me--and her encouraging me--that helped take me there.

When I was in high school, She actually gave me the key chain she won at Eastern Connecticut State. She had her college softball ring on from when they won the 1990 Division III National Softball Championship and she encouraged me and told me that she wanted me to have that same experience, that I could win a championship too. She said, "You could have something like this," pointing to her championship ring.

Dawn came to the final game we were in at the tournament. We lost the game. Even so, I knew it was going to be okay. As Dawn had said to me before: "Shoot for the moon, and if you don't quite make it you are still amongst the stars."

It is important to remember that the journey towards your goal is actually just as valuable as the goal itself. This is something that I learned from Dawn which I always carry with me.

However, through Dawn's impact on me I realized I had a bigger dream for myself beyond sports—although I came really close to all that she had envisioned for me in my athletic career, she let me know it was all okay regardless of what had happened on the court.

Today, I am a high school counselor and my whole job is to help kids. Looking back, I can really see what a special relationship Dawn and I forged during that time. I know now through my own work that you can't always have that connection—or plan for it. It just happens.

Another amazing thing about Dawn is also that she forms lasting bonds. I was even a nanny to her children in the summers when I was in college. We remain close friends today.

She told me when I had my first child to be prepared because it was an unreal kind of love. Of course, she was right.

When you go to Dawn's house, as I did when we had a reunion of sorts about three years ago, you'll find magical positive reminders in the form of quotes everywhere. It is clear that she, too, has to work at her positive mindset.

What is so special to me is that I know Dawn always has my back regardless of time and space and I have hers. Having a good mentor can change the trajectory of your life. I should know because that is exactly what Dawn did, and continues to do, for me.

Wow, I am absolutely humbled by Morgan's words. They also make me happier than I ever thought possible. Not because I want any type of "heroine" stature. Quite the contrary. To me, when I hear a story like that, it's a good indicator that I am doing an effective job in my DM role.

It also makes me step back and remember the people who have played an integral role in my own success and my own struggles…the people who have been Designated Motivators for me.

Who Are *Your* Designated Motivators?

*"Great leaders inspire people to have confidence
in themselves."* — Eleanor Roosevelt

I have been extremely fortunate to have many people impact and
motivate me. I will celebrate those people throughout this book as
examples of how we all need at least one DM and how using the
example of others around us can help us become better DMs ourselves.

Before I share with you the impact of one of my earliest DM influencers
on me, I want to be clear about something:

While this book is about my Designated Motivator philosophy, it is not
about **me**—I wrote it for *you*, so that you can take *your* real life experiences
and your desire to make a positive and lasting impact in the world and
use your Designated Motivator super power to leave people better than
they were and cause your own #MotivationMovement.

What being a DM means to you is going to be different than how I think
about it, but the fundamental mindset, skills and positive outcomes are
going to be the same. This, my fellow DM, is the magic at the heart of
our #MotivationMovement.

Whether you act as a DM to transform the dynamics of a family unit,
drastically improve the engagement of an employee, or help a friend or
acquaintance overcome an issue or problem, never forget that adopting
and sharing the DM philosophy is your superpower that can turn the
"impossible" into an amazing reality for your organization, your team,
your family and your own life.

If you really feel that you are not DM material on this level, I highly encourage you to use this book to be your own DM so you can also achieve great things for yourself that will have a positive impact on others. Then, please, pass it along to your family, friends, colleagues--the people you believe can act as external DMs to help others and create positive change on a larger scale in this world.

My First Experiences with the Power of a DM: My Dad & My Coach

The best way I know how to help you do the DM work you need and want to do is to use parts of my own story. I'll use these perspectives on the outcomes that my own DMs have helped to bring about so that you can gain insights and inspiration to do the same in your world.

In fact, I was extremely fortunate growing up because I had the best example of a DM right under my own roof, in my dad, who is the perfect first example of a DM.

My dad worked at Pratt & Whitney in the days of labor strikes. He was a foreman and his guys would be on the picket line. My dad refused to cross the line and instead set up a cot and slept there until the strike was over.

He was gritty, determined, supportive and a true leader. His "guys" as he would call them looked up to him. He would go to bat for them all day long. But I can promise you those guys worked their asses off for him. He happened to not only be a leader but was a DM himself. Through his example, and the actions he showed toward his team, he motivated them with his loyalty, his belief in them, and the fact that he always had their backs.

The other exposure I had to someone acting as a DM for me was in my days as a student athlete at Eastern Connecticut State University.

The example set by Jeffrey Anderson was another pivotal experience on my path to becoming a DM. As a coach, he was 100% our DM.

In fact, he was my own DM before I even realized what was happening. In fact, he acted in this capacity to get me on the softball team. He recognized my ability to lift others up through my use of humor and crazy antics even then. He must have sensed the power of having someone like me on a team so he invited me to join the softball team in spite of the fact there were many better players already on it.

"You're fun, " he told me. "The team needs that."

For the first season, I primarily pinched hit runs, but for other batters and warmed up the pitchers I fully, I truly embraced my role. I brought spirit and spunk—plus lots of humor to the team.

Coach Anderson always encouraged all of us, telling us to never give up, and he always had motivating words for us to keep us coming back for more. This made me want to do more, be more and achieve more as an individual and as part of the team.

It's a feeling and a philosophy that has travelled with me along my path for many (many!) years. It's also why I know that today, what typically happens around team sports involving youth players is definitely not providing the same kind of Designated Motivator experience and as such, these young athletes are not able to benefit fully from the value of being involved in competitive sports.

If you have witnessed a more recent sporting event, especially one involving kids, you know what I am talking about.

Picture it: The head coach is typically yelling at the players, oftentimes considering this "motivation". Oh, and forget the parents! They are equally ruthless and self-involved, arguing with coaches and each other about the "fact" that their kid should get playing time. Asking why another kid is playing over their child

I know this is true because I have seen and experienced it firsthand—and I bet you have, too!

The fundamental errors that these "leaders" are making is trying to motivate their athletes using solely their authority, scary statistics and a tough love attitude. What they are missing (and their athletes are paying the price for) is the belief that winning shouldn't be your *only* motivation in the game or in life. Doing your best, being in the moment, and, as I like to say (borrowed from Coach Diana Pepin), always remembering the real "W.I.N." or What's Important Now will take you much, much further to achieving your goals.

It has been my experience that when you have *someone designated* to lifting up each player, taking care of their emotions, helping them manage the ups and downs of life so that it doesn't impact their performance or focus on bigger goals, you are exponentially more likely to have a successful team.

Why We *Really* Need Designated Motivators

I can already anticipate that some people who are introduced to this DM concept may really question it. Especially when it comes to applying the DM Mindset and Skill Set to work teams or to drive employee engagement. They may even ask, "What is the big deal about a DM? Shouldn't everyone just do their damn job and stop whining? You know, suck it up buttercup!"

This is the mindset many of us who are forty years old or older may have. If you are part of this group, you probably remember the days when your teacher would not take any crap from you. If you didn't finish your homework, you got an F. If you were on a sports team and yelled at an umpire, your coach would throw you out of the game and then even bench you for at least one more. And certainly, if you were at work, calling out sick for no reason was a very bad idea.

While there is definitely merit to having rules and respect for systems, teams and corporate entities (Trust me, as an entrepreneur and business owner myself this is critical!), I have also found that you cannot overlook the need to build up your human capital as well as your financial and physical resources.

A DM can literally find and facilitate the most valuable contributions possible in the people who work for and with you. Imagine the ROI, productivity and positive results this kind of superpower can bring to your business, team or other organization.

What's In the #MotivationMovement For You?

"No-one has ever become poor by giving." — Anne Frank

It is normal to ask yourself, "What's in it for me?" when being introduced to a new concept such as the importance of being part of a global #MotivationMovement or playing an active part in it as a DM.

Here's my take on why anyone would want to be a DM or at least adopt the mindset and skill set for their own benefit: Because it is a healthier, happier and infinitely more productive way of being in the world. Hands down. End of story.

Consider these questions:

Do you have the intention every day to make someone sad, angry or depressed? No, of course not, that is ridiculous. Most of us want others to be happy and productive.

Do you enjoy being around happy people or mad people? That's a no-brainer, everyone wants to surround themselves with happy people.

Would you rather have people who feel valued and open to new possibilities or those who feel hopeless and unmotivated working with you or on your team? I think we all know the answer to that one! You are much more likely to get the business, sport and group results you are looking for if you have people who fit the first description, right?

For those of you who need the scientific-based argument, here are the facts: Research has proven that just a simple smile can change your life—now imagine what sharing your smile could do if you used it more often in your daily life, especially in your interactions with other people.

The core characteristics I believe natural Designated Motivators possess, such as positivity, optimism, empathy, respect, caring for others and self-love, have proven, positive psychological and organizational benefits.

Many of these characteristics are intrinsic traits. When it comes to motivation, there must be something inside you that drives a passion to perform in whatever activity, job, or environment that you are a part of. When you get up in the morning and are excited about what you do and how you can affect others so that they feel the same way it is, well, magical. This is the very definition of being a motivator, as the Merriam-Webster Dictionary clearly spells out [Pun intended!]:

a. Motivation: One that motivates or impels someone or something, a subconscious motivator of behavior
b. A factor or situation that causes people to feel motivated to do something
c. A person who motivates others

In other words, anyone who can motivate another person to move and perform physically or mentally in a positive direction is a motivator. The results of a *Designated* Motivator can be extraordinary. I believe that every athletic team, business team, medical team, family team and any other group of individuals *MUST* have a carefully chosen motivator to be successful.

The Difference Between Being an Effective Motivator and Practicing "Good" Behavior

I want to be clear on something that is often confused with the mindset, skills and ability to actually motivate others as a DM. Learned "good" behaviors such as things like saying, "Thank you." "Please." "You're Welcome." and common courteous actions such as opening a door for someone and taking out the trash without being asked are things we learn (hopefully) at home. These actions are not necessarily native to your personality but rather teachings from caring adults in our lives. This behavior is fundamentally different than motivation.

To me, the person who is a motivator is someone who has an inherent, innate, intuitive and native ability to engage with others to help them overcome obstacles and achieve meaningful goals.

Based on these abilities, you can see that being a DM is not necessarily something you can teach, unless the person you are attempting to motivate has the willingness to absorb the lessons. Case in point being, those Negative Nellie people out there who believe everything is awful and it will never get better, or the person who has zero self-esteem that requires positive words and affirmations in order to get up in the morning.

The defining characteristic of a DM in my opinion is their ability to turn the negative into the positive. Now don't get me wrong, even the most positive people need someone to motivate *them* from time to time... however, fundamentally, to be an effective DM you need to keep focused on finding the light within yourself, others and the situation at hand, in order to facilitate the move to a higher level of thinking, acting and achieving.

Another key characteristic of a DM, is laughter. I am sure you have heard the science behind how good laughter is for you and everyone around you! If you haven't here's the brief 4-1-1: Laughter has been proven to increase the level of infection-fighting antibodies and boost the level of immune cells.

In this time of the rise of infectious diseases, more than ever, we should be laughing a ton! Think about someone in your life who you always look forward to talking to or hanging out with. What type of person are they? Are they happy, sad, funny, or boring? Well, I can say that I am all in on happiness and fun. People respond to this kind of encouraging demeanor, in my opinion, more so than the in your face authority-based "motivation" we see so many places these days.

Now that you know a little bit about my DM philosophy and the "secret" superpower we can all use to improve life for ourselves and others, let's start tapping into your own inner DM by exploring the key responsibilities inherent in it.

Wait, what? Is that what you are thinking when we talk about DM *responsibilities*? Relax! This is not another "obligation" we are talking about here. It's just three key takeaways which are fundamental to the DM philosophy and can help guide you along your own journey to discovering the Designated Motivator within you.

Discovering the Designated Motivator Within

"Helping one person might not change the whole world,
but it could change the world for one person." — Unknown

Leave people better than you found them. This is my life mantra—and it's the reason why I wanted to write this book. I bet you feel it, too, on some level of your consciousness and that's what drew you to this book (Well, that and my picture on the cover, LOL!). How can I be so sure? Because I know that I am not alone in my belief that the ultimate gift that any of us can give or receive is the realization of human potential.

I also believe, however, that too few of us actually participate in or facilitate this exchange on a daily basis—but if we did, what a world-changer that would be! Do you agree, but are unsure about how you can play a part? If so, I am so glad we have connected through this book, because by the end of it you'll be armed and ready to inspire action in others by interacting in the world as a DM.

Helping others embrace their own greatness and motivating them to actively use it to achieve things beyond their limiting beliefs is the driving force of my life. And I know I am not the only one who feels this stirring in their soul.

In fact, I think that most of us, deep inside, have the desire to do something meaningful with our lives. Self-help gurus often refer to this as our purpose and there are millions of people who are actively seeking to understand what their purpose is. If you have already identified what your purpose is and you are living it, then you are very lucky indeed.

I know that I feel very fortunate to understand what my purpose is--to be a Designated Motivator (or DM), which I define as:

An individual who has the passion and ability to give others the greatest gift of all: the realization and mobilization of their true potential. Someone who uses a specific mindset and skill set to empower others to believe in themselves so they can achieve at higher levels than they thought were possible.

As anyone who has "experienced" me in their life knows, I do things at two levels - not at all or 1000%. There is no middle ground for me. That's why I have honed my motivational skills to be not just a Designated Motivator, but an *Ultimate* Designated Motivator. This has been the place where I choose to focus my energy because this is the impact I want to have in the world and on other people.

If you also feel the urge and passion to help others realize their own gifts and true potential then you, too, have the calling to be a Designated Motivator. Perhaps you have never thought about it in these terms before, you just know that encouraging and empowering others to be better versions of themselves is worth what you want and need to do.

You may have to level-up your Designated Motivator skill set in order to really have the impact you need to have on others.

What do I mean by that in the practical sense? I am glad you asked! Let's start with those three key responsibilities we spoke of at the end of the previous chapter.

The Three Key Responsibilities of a Designated Motivator

1. Encourage unconditionally.
2. Provide emotional, physical, and psychological support.
3. Cause a positive transformative effect in another person on a mental, emotional, spiritual and/or physical level.

I highly encourage the use of humor, crazy antics, costumes (a personal favorite tactic) and more to motivate your peeps, the above responsibilities will go a long way to helping you be an amazing DM.

I truly believe that having more DMs in the world will lead to amazing increases in productivity, effectiveness, happiness, self-fulfillment and people feeling fulfilled by the actual accomplishment of their life and career goals.

I know this is true because I have seen it happen one person at a time in my own world where I strive every day to be a DM at home, at work, on the softball field (More about that later!), and every time I interact with someone.

I am simply driven to do what I can to help people become better versions of themselves and to tap what I can see they are capable of, but they may not be already aware of.

Now *that* is what having a lasting legacy is all about. In my humble opinion, this is one of the greatest secrets that a proportionately few people know...being a DM is a powerful gift that can change the world at a fundamental level and one that I believe many more people could harness for a greater good if they only had someone to be their DM in the process and the tools to make it happen.

If your heart sings at the prospect of tapping into your own DM powers and joining our #MotivationMovement, then stay with me on the following pages because I will be your DM right here, right now. I want to leave you better than when you first started this book and empower your own greatness, because I know it is there, just waiting to be unleashed.

In this book you'll find the fundamentals of being a DM, so that together we can encourage, support and transform the people we meet on our journey and use the DM Toolkit each day to put our passion into practice. The idea is to create a lasting, meaningful legacy not only for ourselves, but for all the people, families, organizations and other groups we have the privilege to engage with, whether it is for just a brief period or over the course of a lifetime.

Of course, I understand not everyone is a direct DM, you may feel that this is an important role best passed along to someone you feel has that inner calling which is stronger than your own. That's okay, I just ask that you do share the concept and tools of the DM with them so that you can contribute to our #MotivationMovement in the way that is most comfortable and natural for you.

The Designated Motivator Mindset

"Whether you think you can or think
you can't, you are right." — Henry Ford.

While I consider my own story to be pretty amazing, I think the most exciting part of you investing the time to read it, learn from it, and apply the principles in it, is that you, or someone you determine is a natural DM, will transform to fill the role. In doing so, you have the potential to transform yourself and others in all areas of your daily life from your family to your careers, to the organizations you are involved in.

In a nutshell, when you decide to become a Designated Motivator you will have the opportunity to change the lives of others around you in many, and often, surprising ways.

I know, I know, some of you may be thinking, "Nope, I am not a 'motivator type' this is not for me." I would argue that everyone can choose to embrace the responsibilities and the behaviors of a DM, even if they aren't "a natural" or at least, they don't consider themselves to be.

For example, you may own a large company, be the leader in a work project, the coach of a sports team (at any level), or the head of a surgical team. In any of these positions it isn't necessarily the responsibility of the *designated leader* to be the *Designated Motivator.* Rather, the individual who has the key characteristics of a motivator, should be designated as such. And if you don't think you already have one on your team, be motivated enough to find one!

Who knows, the next amazing DM who chooses to adopt the specific principles below into their mindset could be you...or someone you haven't even met yet!

You may be wondering, "Are some people born to motivate others? Are they just naturally gifted with the ability to be optimistic and look on the bright side of life, bringing rainbows and puppies everywhere they go?"

I want you to remember as we delve deeper into the fundamental mind shifts and behavior patterns associated with becoming a Designated Motivator (at whatever level you choose) that we all need to fill our own cups first. It's akin to putting on your own oxygen mask before helping the person next to you put on theirs.

This point is absolutely critical.

Being a DM does not mean you should try to substitute your help for appropriate mental health care or the advice of a healthcare professional. This applies to you—and the people you come into contact with in the world. While being a DM is very powerful, it is a philosophy and a method of interacting with others as the opportunities to encourage, empower and enlighten them present themselves. It is not intended to be a substitute for appropriate professional care.

If someone you know needs more support than you can provide please help them get it quickly. Mental health is just as important as physical health...if not more so. We need to respect this fact and take appropriate action when we or someone we know is struggling.

What Being a Designated Motivator Is *Not*

You may be thinking, "Yes, I could be a DM. I like the idea of helping other people achieve goals and also benefit from everyone around me being more positive and productive but being happy and encouraging all of the time, it's not really my thing...not something that is possible for me."

To this, I say, "Hold. The. Phone."

Being a Designated Motivator is not like being a perpetual Pollyanna. I can tell you right now that while I am able to be an effective DM 95% of the time—because I work at applying and living the fundamentals of the DM mindset (we will explore these together in a minute) *every day*—there are times when I need some time off from the role. And I give myself permission to take a break from being the one who is lifting everyone else up and practice self-care.

Let's be real, no one is going to be a DM 100% of the time. We all need support and encouragement—I will be the first in line to say that! When I feel defeated or that I could have made a better choice in the way I treated a situation, I recognize that sometimes I need someone to help me pick myself back up instead of beating myself up.

Sometimes it is another person, oftentimes I ask my internal DM to take on a gentler tone so I can take a mental break. Yes, I have definitely learned that sometimes all I need is to simply binge-watch Netflix and give myself the chance to recharge my own batteries so I can regain my DM mindset and get it (and all of the physical manifestations of it) ready to fire again.

So what is the DM mindset? I have identified these six fundamental beliefs that I believe are the foundation of thinking like a DM:

1. **Kindness is Kryptonite** – Yes, what the world needs now is love, sweet love—and there is too little of it! Kindness is one of the greatest healing powers we can share with another human and it costs nothing!

Kindness can take on so many forms—from simply not saying something critical or giving someone grace for an error they made, to actually giving someone a tangible token of your appreciation for who they are and what they do.

I know you likely already try to operate with and think with kindness most of the time, but I find that sometimes it is easier said than done. As a Designated Motivator you need to remember that kindness is your kryptonite and that you can be the soft place where someone that you are motivating can come and experience the type of kindness they need, when they need it.

2. **Empathy is Empowering** – Being a DM requires that you can have empathy for others and their situation. For most of us, just knowing that someone else is trying to put themselves in our shoes will make us feel less alone. Practicing and showing empathy for others' situations is empowering for the person going through a tough time. We want to show them that we understand, we are on their team and we can help them transcend the problem into a more positive reality going forward.

Psychologists Daniel Goleman and Paul Ekman identified three components of empathy: Cognitive, Emotional and Compassionate. They define them this way:

Cognitive: Taking time to know how the other person feels and what they are thinking.

Emotional: Allowing yourself to physically feel the emotions of another person.

Compassionate: Once we understand a person's situation and point of view, we use our emotional investment in them as the driver for helping them through it.

Ideally as a DM, you can employ all three facets of empathy to empower change in another person. Most importantly, for our #MotivationMovement to have a deep and lasting impact we need empathy to build stronger relationships and trust with our "Motivatees" (Trust me, it's a word—I made it up!).

3. **Pain Can Be Powerful** – No one gets through this life without experiencing some level of pain. As a Designated Motivator, it is likely that you will help your Motivatee move past some form of pain. Pain can be debilitating, but it can also be—with the right mindset—a motivator to take us to the next level that we need to progress to. If you can adopt this mindset both personally and when you are motivating others, it can also be a very powerful force in your life.

4. **Positivity is Priceless** – As I said before, being a DM is not being an oblivious optimist—it is about helping others see that they can overcome their own challenges and perceived limitations to achieve greater things.

Without a positive mind set—one that you help your Motivatee create—you will struggle to succeed as a DM. Helping others create and maintain positive beliefs is a pivotal part of your DM role. If you are looking for your own DM, they should help you define any roadblocks you have mentally to becoming rich with positivity. Positivity truly is priceless because it fuels the passion for achieving all of our possibilities and fulfilling the highest expression of our potential.

5. **Gifts Are Given to All** – One of the mindsets that is inherent in almost every DM is the belief that everyone on this earth has a gift that is tied to their ultimate purpose. Sadly, many, many people either a) don't realize this and/or b) never appreciate and use their gift fully.

The vast majority of humans have a treasure trove of gifts from creativity to analytical skills to hands-on abilities that can all be used to do amazing things. As a DM, you likely have an innate ability to recognize people's gifts and your work is to bring them to the belief and desire to utilize them fully to accomplish a given goal or series of goals. This ability is one of your many, many gifts.

6. **Focus on Forward** – This may be one of the most important parts of being a DM. The ability to help others move out of past pain and pessimism and into a future that is ripe with possibility and achievement.

As a DM, we need to keep our Motivatees looking and moving forward to unwrap their gifts and maximize their potential. Getting stuck in the past is the kiss of death to all forms of motivation.

Keep yourself and the people who you are motivating focused forward with all the things that they have to look forward to. All of the things they have still to achieve and all of the potential within them. Possibility is a picture you need to paint for people and for yourself.

When you can visualize what could be, instead of ruminating on what was or what is, you unlock one of the most powerful forms of motivation there is.

Our thoughts lead to our actions and in order to act like a true Designated Motivator it is essential to think like one —starting with the mindsets we've discussed above. Working to adopt these ways of framing life and all of our experiences can put you on a powerful path which can take your DM abilities to new levels, helping your Mentees achieve their goals as well.

It's been said that if you can change your mind, you can change your life. This is so true, especially when it comes to adopting and applying the Designated Motivator Mindset above!

I can think of no better way for me to illustrate this fact than to take you back with me to the spring of 2019 when my life—and the lives of 25 Lady Warriors team members changed forever. This is the only time in this book that we will be doing a flashback instead of focusing forward, in keeping with The Designated Motivator Mindset!

Everything Happens For A Reason

"The most important thing is to try and inspire people so that
they can be great in whatever they want to do." — Kobe Bryant

In the spring of 2018, I was asked to represent the Anderson Family by presenting the Jeffrey W Anderson Memorial Award, in honor of my late coach, Jeff Anderson who passed away in the fall after my senior year in college. The award is presented to an individual for their devotion to, and support of, the Eastern softball program, as exemplified by Anderson's own dedication and love for the program and all student-athletes.

The Anderson family could not be present to give out the award so I stepped in to represent them. I was honored to present the award with Diana Pepin, the Head Coach of the NCAA Women's Collegiate Fastpitch Softball team at Eastern Connecticut State University, who happened to be one of my former teammates "back in the day". She also remains a really good friend, I attribute this in part to our shared history.

In 1990, she and I were members of the Division III National Championship Softball team. Playing on that team was one of the most transformative experiences of my life.

Coach Pepin is an amazing coach and I was honored by her request for me to sit in the dugout for the game. In the back of my mind I was thinking, "OMG, these kids have no idea what was coming their way!"

Anyone who knows me accepts the fact that I am an absolute lunatic when it comes to business, life, sports, family, etc. Oh yeah, basically I have a 100 to zero mentality. This, as applied to the dugout experience, means that the young women playing ball that day probably left the field wondering who I was—this crazy person who had unofficially joined their team. It was super exciting for me because "we" (Of course I was part of that team already in my mind!) won both games of the double header.

Through this process, the young women on that team experienced a small glimpse of what was to come, which surprised even me, because at that point, no plans had been officially made for the future of my coaching career. I left those kids stunned and asking themselves, who is this crazy person anyway?

I didn't have time to coach a team , anyway, given my crazy busy work and family life. But in hindsight, I sure am glad that I tapped into my DM capabilities and *made* the time to coach the team—because what happened next was an experience that transformed my life and those of an entire team of people, forever changing us for the better. I asked Coach Pepin to provide a little more insight into how it all went down, from a Designated Motivator Perspective:

The Impact of a Designated Motivator

Coach Diana Pepin

"Dawn's energy is contagious and she really is the good cop to my bad cop—she motivates us all on a daily basis."

Dawn and I played softball together in college and we've remained good friends through all of these years.

I am currently the head coach of the Lady Warriors softball team at Eastern Connecticut State University. Each member of the coaching staff has a different relationship with the girls and with each other. The quality of these relationships are key to our success as a team.

For example, I am the hard ass and Dawn is the lighter side of our partnership. She always brings levity to every situation which is important. It helps keep us focused and at ease as a team.

Dawn's two daughters are about the same age as many of our players which really helps her relate to them. It helps her decipher what our players need. She knows when to push and when to give the girls some space to decompress. It's the perfect foil to me who is always wanting to drive forward a little harder.

I have learned from Dawn the importance of having that balance. Even though her style is light at heart, she brings a lot of drive and determination out of the team members. She has a skill for opening herself up to help others and has literally talked some girls off a ledge. Needless to say, she genuinely loves the girls and they feel that and the girls love her, too.

Unleashing My Designated Motivator

"If you can get fired up, people will come from miles to watch you burn." — Nelson Millardspeaks

When I think back to the college softball season of 2019, I remember how nervous I was in the beginning. I really had no idea what I was going to be able to offer to the Eastern Connecticut State University Lady Warrior team as a volunteer assistant coach.

The truth was I had been away from the field for a long time. This makes how I found myself back on it in an "official" capacity even more amazing—especially because the opportunity (one that I almost turned down) turned out to be the pivotal experience which unleashed the full force of my own Designated Motivator.

It was at the close of the 2018 season that I had the opportunity to present the Jeff Anderson Memorial Award.

At the end of the ceremony, Head Coach, Diana Pepin, looked at me and said, "Hey, you want to stay and hang out in the dugout for a bit?"

Coach Pepin and I were teammates back in the 1990s when we won the 1990 National Championship. This created a lifelong bond, the kind that you never ever forget.

I really missed the days of playing because they were such an important part of my life and had such a major impact on me. It was that impact that pulled me to go back to the dugout that day.

33

As I walked across the field to get there, I remembered the days when our coach, if we weren't hitting the ball or performing well, would take the bats and he would throw them out on the ground. Then he would take some eye drops (real or pretend) and spray them all over the bats so they would wake up. We would then get on a hitting rally and just kick ass. I smiled at the memory then laughed to myself, because something inside of me had just sparked in a major way.

I sat in the dugout for about a minute during the game that day. The players weren't really hitting the ball very well, so I got up and started trying to encourage them. And, of course, if you know me, you know I am a bit psychotic, it's my normal state.

True to myself, I was jumping around the dugout. I grabbed the bats. I threw them all on the ground. And I kicked them around.

"Wake up those bats!" I just started going crazy. And the kids kind of got into it. I think they liked it, but they were likely thinking, "This is just weird."

It was quite a contrast to Coach Pepin who is so steadfast and driven when she coaches. The players were not really sure what to do with me. They, did however, begin to understand what to do as a team. They ended up rallying, coming back, winning the game and the double header.

That day was a really impactful one for me. I really felt like, "Oh, man, I think I've just passed it on." This is what our coach used to say, "Pass it on." That's what I did. It was super fun. Then I moved on with my life, bragged about it for about a week, not about me, but just about how fun it was to be in the dugout and be able to give back a little bit to the program that changed my life.

Breakfast—and Back to the Ball Games?

Let's fast forward to the fall of 2018, and my buddy Pepin shoots me a text that said, "Hey, let's go get some breakfast."

We went down to Blondie's, our usual spot. When we sat down, she said, "Hey, what do you think about coaching?"

"Oh, man, are you crazy?" I responded, then provided a list of excuses for why I couldn't do it. From my work (I'm a CPA) to my worries about what value I could bring to the team. "There's tax season. I don't remember the rules. I don't know. What good could I be for your team? I mean, don't you usually bring someone onto your team for a reason that would actually make your team better?"

Pepin responded bluntly: "You have enthusiasm. You're psychotic. And I think you could really bring the kids a whole different energy."

She was persuasive, that is for sure. It's always been an important part of who I am, to lift up young people and motivate them to explore all of their possibilities. It was this desire that drove me to take on what was going to be a significant challenge.

"Well, let me think about it. I mean, I do have tax season, and it's really crazy already, so let me think about it," I said, even though inside I was already practically bursting at the opportunity to put my DM desires to good use.

I practiced self-restraint, though, because as I mentioned at the beginning of this book, when I do something I am all in! I thought about it for a couple of weeks, then I called Coach Pepin.

"Absolutely, I'll do it. I'll do the best I can to be at as many practices and games as I can. But just understand, tax season takes precedent," I said.

"Okay, cool, I'll take it," Pepin responded. She's persistent, there's no doubt about that.

The next week, I received the letter. I was officially a volunteer assistant coach of the 2019 Lady Warriors softball team.

2019: The Pivot Point

"Why fit in when you were born to stand out?" — Dr. Seuss

It's the start of the 2019 season, I am on my way to the first team meeting. I'm so nervous it is insane. I decide the best antidote to my apprehension is to just be myself. So that is what I do.

As expected, after a few minutes of me being me, the players are looking confused. I can tell they are thinking that I'm weird. I don't care because I am in full-on DM mode.

Another one of my life mantras is: It's just who I am, man. By the way, if you don't already have a phrase like this that helps you stay true to who your authentic self is, I highly encourage you to find one that you find is true for you.

Gradually, however, an amazing thing happened. The team began to accept and appreciate my wacky ways. Julia, who was a freshman at the time, summed it up by saying: "She's just like Melissa McCarthy." And I was like, "Yep, I get that all the time."

It was my total lack of inhibition and my willingness to put myself out there in front of a group of accomplished and high-achieving young women that was the icebreaker in many ways.

They began to understand and accept that, yes, Coach Brolin is psychotic, then we got down to the business of becoming the best team that we could be.

That was the goal. It wasn't about the winning or the glory for the players or anyone on the coaching staff. It was all about transforming the individual players into the best versions of themselves and creating a cohesive team that was better together than they were apart.

Finding My Place as a Designated Motivator

That season we went to Florida for spring break. This trip was when I really got to know the kids. I was in charge of one van as the driver. As you can imagine, this arrangement allowed me to get to know the kids who travelled with me quickly. It was still awkward; I won't lie about that. I still wasn't sure if they were going to buy into my crazy energy or not.

During the trip, my DM antenna went up and I really began to zone in on kids who weren't performing well. I wanted to shake them out of the status quo and do something weird to take them from where they were to a whole different level of performance.

So, never one to underestimate the power of candy, I decided to leverage my love of mini chocolate eggs to help one player who had been struggling when she went up to bat.

Just to be clear, I like the little hard candy mini eggs, not the ones with the cream stuff in the middle, those are nasty, in my opinion. I bought the preferred variety of eggs at a convenience store and brought them to our next practice. The team member I had zoned in on to share them with played right into my plans!

"I love those," she said, eyeing the treats.

"When you go to bat, I'll open the bag," I told her.

I had decided that when she was almost ready to bat, I would give her a mini egg before she went up to play. So that's what I did and she eagerly accepted the candy.

What happened next was actually pretty cool, given that she was our fourth batter, which is the most critical hitter in the lineup. She was a Power Hitter but she was having trouble when she was under pressure.

Suddenly, after receiving a mini egg (If yellow didn't work, then we switched to pink or blue.) she was crushing the ball! She was a rockstar!

We created the belief that it was the candy that was the reason she was suddenly performing so well, but we all secretly knew it was her ability to embrace FUN and use it to diffuse the high-pressure situation which made all the difference.

The treat helped to shift her mindset to: Sure, I am up to bat, but guess what? So what? Stop thinking so hard about it and start having fun with it.

Soon, the candy eggs before she went to bat became a thing just between us.

Not long after this point was when I was able to really get to know each member of the team: Their past, their present and their personality. I wanted to understand what they had gone through and what their life had been like to that point. This is where it started to get really deep and I went into my full DM mode on steroids.

I was able to look into their eyes and give them a message of, "Listen, I know you've got shit going on at home. But let's focus on this. And then after the game, we're going to get things going. We're going to talk. We're going to figure out how we can at least keep your mind positive, even though I know you're going through some stuff at home, or you're just having some troubles personally in various areas."

This is where I went from assistant coach to taking it to a different level of connection as the DM.

I knew during these deeper moments that my job was to be a Designated Motivator. That is, my job was to motivate these kids and help them believe there was more in them than they even knew, and that they were capable of things they never thought that they were capable of before.

Inspiring Others to Become Designated Motivators

Sarah Pisanelli, The Candy Egg Girl!

I met Dawn during my junior year when I played shortstop on the 2019 Lady Warriors team.

We had never seen anything like Dawn in the dugout! She was a crazy lady but her antics worked to help us relax and keep motivated even when things were tough. She was like a second mom at times, too.

Dawn not only helped me with enthusiasm and encouragement on and off the field, but the experience also inspired me to become a DM, too.

What I learned from Dawn is invaluable, especially now as I coach my own team of girls. One of the most important things she taught me is that every team needs someone who will help to pick people up when they are down and help them celebrate when they are on top. That's what I hope I can pass along myself as a coach and as I go through my life.

The Ultimate Designated Motivator: Putting Aspiration Into Action

"There's no need to be perfect to inspire others. Let people get inspired by how you deal with your imperfections." — Ziad K. Abdeinour

Reflecting back on 2018, the team had a less than .500 average. In 2019, we had the same kids on the same team, with one player graduating and one incoming. The incoming players we call the newcomer class. It's a freshmen class, but we still call them newcomers.

So newcomers come in, but the same team otherwise, comes together, and so, they're figuring, yeah, it's going to be the same old, same old year after year. We're just a .500 team. Although Eastern has a history of championships, these ladies just didn't feel it. They didn't know the passion you needed to achieve this higher level. They didn't know the drive and determination that it takes to be a champion.

However, Coach Pepin and I were determined to teach them about it. We helped our players take that next step that season.

It was on my mind and in my heart to help this team experience what we had experienced back in 1990. When we won that National Championship. When we were the most talented team. Or were we the most talented team?

I really don't think we were the most talented team back in 1990. I can say that because I played left field, and I was the one who scored the winning run. That wasn't my strong suit--usually. No, it wasn't about skill that year, it was about passion, and it was about drive. It was about commitment, dedication and teamwork. As you have probably heard, and as I firmly believe, there is no "I" in team. All we had were our inner gifts which allowed us to win that season. That was it, period. Everyone gave 110% of themselves no matter what. And so, that was what I wanted to infuse into that team in 2019.

I know that our win wasn't because of Dawn Brolin. It was because of someone who made the decision to impart the spirit and provide the necessary skills of success to these kids—a Designated Motivator who can teach them that anything really is possible.

That's not something you just read in a book, because a lot of that stuff is bullshit. It's a fact that if you can convince yourself and believe that your team has everything they need to be successful (even when no one else believes it) and if you make a commitment to believing in it, you can accomplish absolutely anything that you put your mind to.

It was with this belief and unwavering dedication that Assistant Coach Mark Correia, Tom Madeira, myself and Head Coach Pepin worked to convince our team that they could win a national championship.

The Power of Being True to Your Inner Designated Motivator

Assistant Coach Mark Correia

The night after my first softball practice with Dawn, I went home and told my girls, "You will not believe the woman who I am coaching with. She is like Melissa McCarthy! She looks like her but most of all she acts like her, too!"

Of course, we all found out that Melissa McCarthy has nothing on Dawn! Her antics are wild and they help to bring out the best in all of us on the team.

Dawn is the perfect complement to our awesome foursome of coaches. Diana is the disciplinarian, I am in the middle, Tom is empowering and then there's Dawn who is always out there doing whatever she needs to do to make everyone laugh and be their best. She is the perfect Designated Motivator for our team and I can imagine she is the same in her business relationships, too.

From going on a road trip dressed like Melissa McCarthy from the airplane scene in the movie "Bridesmaids," to showing up for the first practice after the pandemic practice protocol was announced in a full hazmat suit, Dawn has elevated the team experience to a level which has created new opportunities for everyone involved.

She inspires all of us with her confidence and makes sure that everyone is having fun. You can't underestimate that given the amount of stress that so many of these kids are under these days. She is like a second mom to a lot of girls who are away from home and often facing academic, social and financial pressures. She is a great option for them to turn to for motivation and to get through the hard stuff.

Eyes on the Prize:
The National College Softball Championship

By all accounts, our team had a successful season. We were doing very, very well, but we needed to take it to the absolute next level if we were going to win the Little East Tournament, which was the goal at the time. Coach Pepin and I always had the National Tournament in the backs of our mind because we believed these kids could get there.

We knew if we were going to win the Little East Tournament, we needed to help the team believe they were capable of it.

We knew that we had to do it one pitch at a time, one inning at a time. You can never look forward to what ifs. It's what is happening now.

Our motto for the team was W.I.N., not win the game, but What's Important Now? This is because Coach Pepin believes that you cannot always be looking forward to things. You have to look at the present and stay in the moment in order to achieve greatness through concerted effort.

This is what we taught the kids, and that's been Coach Pepin's lifelong philosophy. It's led her, and those who practice it with her, to much success.

The Curse of the Field

"This is your time! Now go out there and take it!" — Herb Brooks

We are playing Plymouth State in our last regular season game. Call us superstitious, but we actually believe the field is cursed against Eastern Connecticut State University. We lost that double header, right before the Little East Conference Tournament (LEC).

We don't play at home for the LEC because we needed to beat Plymouth twice to be the host of the tournament. So we had to go to UMass Dartmouth and be an away team. I think we were even seed number three. I really don't remember those kinds of details because they're irrelevant. I am focused on the inner work of motivation, not the external gratification of a win.

When we get to the tournament, we're just having fun. We're the underdog, and there's nothing better than going into a tournament as an underdog. Underdog meaning not ranked number one.

Why would I say this? Because it shifts the focus from an external gratification of winning to the feeling of playing in the mindset of, "We went in there, we kicked @** and we took names." This is because we believed and we knew that we were having fun. As such, we were all motivated to achieve the exact same goal. We also knew that it took every single person on the team, no matter what their role was, to win that tournament.

And win we did. As champions of the LEC, we then went on to the Regional Tournament. We were, of course, the underdogs in the

Regional Tournament because no one even expected us to win the Little East Conference Tournament. We have to go away to Tufts, T-U-F-T-S. Let's see how "Tuff" they are, right?

We ended up winning that tournament. We won that Regional Tournament, which was absolutely not expected, either.

Also not expected was the great honor I received that day....the kids voted me the person who really made the difference in that game. Talk about a memory I will treasure forever!

We keep going through the tournament season. Again, we were on fire. We're just bringing craziness into the game. By this point we can see it's working. The players are really starting to believe in their abilities to be a winning team.

The Underdogs

In what seems like a blink of an eye, it's time for the Super Regional Tournament. As it turns out, a team in another region lost their game. Not just any team...it was the host team. You have to apply to be a host team. However, because we were the team that was higher ranked and won more games, we ended up being the host team. So we got to play at home for the Super Regional Tournament.

Again, we're the underdogs. We won the whole tournament. That's a win at the Super Regional Tournament! Which means that Eastern Connecticut State University is going back to the National Tournament. Absolutely unheard of, it's nowhere on the map, it reminds me of Baylor, when Baylor came through and won the National Championship, and they came out of nowhere. They were a nobody team.

Now, to be clear, Eastern Connecticut State University is not a "nobody" softball program. We've been to the National Tournaments. We've won many Little East Conference Tournaments, many Regional

Tournaments and many National Tournaments. So it wasn't new to the program, but it had been a while. But it was time to bring Eastern into the big leagues and put Eastern back on the map. As we headed to the National Tournament. The team was just like, "Oh. My. Gosh."

There are a lot of rules when you go to a national tournament. This was true even pre-COVID. You have to walk only in certain areas. Only so many people in the dugout and you have to have certain passes to get into certain places. Only particular people can walk you around. And you had to have somebody actually walk you around. It wasn't like you could just wander on your own. Ironically, the coach from the team we beat in the Super Regionals had to be our host. So she had to be the one who walked us around. During this time, we got to know her really well, and she was just an awesome person. It was really fun.

At the national tournament, were ranked eighth. That's the eighth out of eight teams. Were going to play the number one team in the first game. And the kids are saying, "We're just happy to be here." And I'm like, "No, we're happy to be here to win this thing. We're not here to just show up. We're here to win this thing."

During this time there was a lot of emotional management and a lot of mindset management, which is integral to being a Designated Motivator. Another integral skill is focus management where you make sure that the person you are working with is still keeping their eye on the prize, whether that is finishing a project or winning a softball tournament.

We ended up beating the number one team that first day and just blew everybody's mind away. Not our minds though, we were there to win. We were there to play. And we were there to put everything on the field, to leave it absolutely all on the field. And so, that is what we did. We beat that number one team and shook up Division III women's softball, which was awesome. There's nothing better than that, causing an earthquake over a softball game.

No Time for Losers...

Next, we played the team that ended up winning the National Tournament. We played them on a Friday and lost by one run. It was a terrible loss in that we could have won it. We beat ourselves.

I think that's one of the biggest things you need to realize as a DM: For most people, the biggest threat to achieving their goals and dreams is their own self. That's right. They are going to defeat themselves in whatever it is. They put up their own obstacles and their own walls, and your job is to break them down. Break them down with motivation, with encouragement, with purpose, with a focus of, "You can do this!" Fire them up—doing it in ways they never imagined.

Let me share an example of what I mean on that last point:

One of the ways I did it for the team was when we were out of town for away games, we would do a bed check. At the National Tournament I took this practice of "lighting the fire within people" up several notches.

Before our trip to the national championship, we had several road trips. On the first one, on our first night at the hotel, I did the bed check with Coach Pepin because she always did it.

That first night I went in and said, "What are you doing? What do you guys have for snacks?" And I would just be crazy and just make them laugh. I wasn't just being silly, though. I had a plan and a purpose because the most important thing you want for anybody who has had a defeat that day is to put them to bed with a positive mindset.

How can you do that? By just acting like an idiot and giving them crazy encouragement that they don't realize even exists.

That's why at the tournaments we went to, I went around wearing costumes. At the Regional Tournament up in Tufts, it had rained out that day, so the kids were kind of down. The perfect opportunity for me to wear my old uniform (Yes, I stole it back in the day, but please don't tell anyone!). So I had my old uniform and let's just say it doesn't fit that great. I also put on one of the kids' batting helmets, and that was my outfit for bed check that night.

This kind of a craziness put the kids in a mindset that they just never imagined was possible. It relieved their anxiety and the tension that we had throughout the day. They went to bed with smiles on their faces, as opposed to a mindset filled with anxiety. A simple but effective tactic for leaving them with a more motivated mindset.

As it turns out, even though we came in third place at the National Tournament, it was an experience of a lifetime, none of us will ever forget it. It changed me—and it changed the other coaches and the players on the team.

And that was my goal: to give them the same experience that I had back in 1990. An experience that we'll never forget: winning a National Championship. Again, it wasn't actually about the win, it was the experience of going to the National Tournaments and being on display and being able to show what you're capable of when you choose to break through the boundaries of your current beliefs.

Leading by Example: The DM Mindset in Action

Sabrina "Sabby" Lemere

Leadership is about a commitment to being on your A-Game. It's also about playing with all your heart and providing motivation for others.

I was a player on both the 2018 and 2019 Eastern Connecticut State University Lady Warriors Team. 2018 was definitely a building year. We were trying to create a more positive and stronger team. In 2019 we were actually able to achieve this—we had some new freshmen who were great players and Dawn Brolin joined as our assistant coach, which took our motivation to a whole new level. She lit a spark within all of us—making us gradually believe that we had within us what we needed to actually go to the National Championship. That was not on our radar before.

Dawn encouraged me to really step into my leadership role as one of the older players. She also created a really incredible motivational vibe for everyone on the team. If someone was down, she would lift them up. Most importantly though, she kept us thinking about what we wanted to achieve, both individually and as a team.

For me, Dawn was definitely a role model and mother figure who always has my back. Before each game, she would give me quote cards to lift my spirits and to remind me that I could do anything I set my mind to.

"You are great!" she would say, even if I had a bad at bat or didn't perform well on the field. She would just tell me, "Don't worry about that, stay focused on the goal." She really kept me focused and positive on and off the field.

When I was a student and even now, as a graduate, I call her for advice and we both call each other just to check in on a regular basis. We are a lot alike in that we both love to motivate people and we don't care if we are loud or look crazy doing it!

Today, I am a physical education and health teacher at a middle school. I also coach the basketball team. Middle school is challenging because the kids are going through so many changes and they relish the fight against being told what to do sometimes.

I apply a lot of what I learned from Dawn as I work with my students and my players. Most importantly, I try to keep them in a positive frame of mind and encourage them to believe in what they can do.

One of the lessons that I took away from my college athletic experience that there isn't really a point of doing something if you aren't happy and motivated to do it. Pump people up and try to see the good in everything. Personally, I know that I can do things that others can't, so I don't take that for granted—and I try to pass that on to my students and other people I meet.

As transformational coach Marissa Peer says, "Once you change your mind, it is forever changed. You never go back to the way you used to be."

From one DM to another—this is what our driving passion is all about— leaving people better than we found them, not for just a moment, but hopefully, for the rest of their lives. All we need are the tools necessary to do it.

That's what I am going to give you in the next section: Your Designated Motivator Toolkit.

I truly believe that the tools we are about to explore, when combined with your own adoption of the Designated Motivator Mindset that we covered earlier, will provide you with everything you need to tap into that DM superpower within you.

I hope that as you read about them, you'll keep a notebook handy so you can add your own ideas for how you can motivate and inspire others to use their gifts to their fullest potential.

Finding Your Designated Motivator Dimensions

"The way we do anything is the way we do everything." — Martha Beck

How you approach being a Designated Motivator is no different. In the Designated Motivator Toolkit section coming up, you'll have a chance to see what kind of Designated Motivator Mindset you have, as well as how you can apply your skills as a DM to work, family and other situations.

For now, simply consider that if you choose to be a DM only for yourself and maybe those close to you, this is wonderful! However, if you are more of the "all in" type of person or even if you just feel that you can do a little more in the world using the DM philosophy then I think you'll appreciate the following insights into how I have seen the amazing impact of the DM philosophy when applied beyond the sports field. Although being a DM in the sports arena is a deep and critical DM dimension for me, there are other areas that I am deeply passionate about as a DM, namely: at home, in the classroom and in my business as a CPA.

Like many of you, the dimensions I named above are the places where I spend a significant amount of time interacting with others on a deeper level. In these places, when we do engage as DMs, we can really help people become better versions of themselves over the long-term.

The results are so rewarding! Imagine the satisfaction and joy of seeing the beneficial outcomes on the special people in your family unit, in your workplace and all of the other places where you are able to lift up and help others appreciate and activate their potential.

For some of us, beyond our families and work, we may have other dimensions where our DM can take the lead as well. These may be at our place of worship, in a service club, or in some other kind of volunteer opportunity. In my case, I also adjunct teach at Eastern Connecticut University, so the classroom is my fourth DM dimension.

To recap, my four primary DM dimensions are family, work, the softball team and teaching. Being engaged and focused as a DM in these areas motivates *me* to get up every morning knowing that I'm going to be able to live my purpose and help others do the same. I share these examples to give you some inspiration for you to determine your own DM Dimensions and go do the important work in them!

Let's start at home, because for most of us, if we are lucky that is where our hearts truly want to do our deepest and best work as DMs. I know I do, and I owe so much to my amazing family members, who you'll get to meet in the coming pages.

The Designated Motivator in the Family: You Get What You Give

Between my husband and my two daughters, Emily and Kayla, who are in their early 20s, there are plenty of days when being a Designated Motivator in our home is, uh, challenging, to say the least. I am not referring only to my own DM experience—my husband Kevin (a saint), is also a bona fide DM, just in a different way than I am. I am introducing you to him here so he can tell you in his own words about some of the ways we keep each other uplifted and doing the best we can on our individual and shared DM journeys.

Like every family we have highs and lows, but one thing is for certain— we all know that when it comes right down to it we have each other's backs—always!

A few examples:

- I was building my accounting practice when I had my two daughters (they are barely a year apart). Not long after they were born, I decided to pursue my master's degree in accounting. We also decided I would be the primary breadwinner and my husband would stay home and look after our girls. As you can imagine, we both had to take on the DM role at different times to lift up and encourage each other in what were very hectic and, at times difficult, life phases.

- Recently, my husband decided to pursue his paralegal degree and we all supported and cheered him on as he took on earning the degree. We were always encouraging him and did our best to relieve him of various household duties so he could focus on his goal.

- Now that my daughters are graduating from college, there have been struggles, especially with social media getting into their heads. This requires ongoing DM deprogramming!

- My daughter, Emily, is in the film industry, and I mean films like movies or in a theater. She's a musical theater major and a film minor, her industry has been destroyed thanks to the COVID-19 pandemic.

  It would be easier as a parent at times to tell her to alter her dreams and go find a more mainstream profession, but I believe she should follow her passion and that she has the gifts to do it!

  In my opinion, being a parent is the most important DM role there is, so I use my DM skills to help Emily keep motivated to take the steps she needs to achieve her goals. Because, as I tell her, "There's something. There's something out there that you're going to do and you're going to do it great because you're a Brolin and that's what we do. When we do things, we do them great, and we do them for a purpose and with a purpose."

  She shall persevere…and find her amazing path, with our entire family providing all of the motivation and support we can give her every step of the way!

As Kevin, my daughters and many others will tell you, truthfully, I am far from perfect in my DM role. I am simply a woman who tries to show up each day and encourage my family and anyone I come in contact with, as best I can. The amazing thing is, the more I use my DM mindset and skill set with them, the more I see it reflected back to me. It is a pay-it-forward kind of thing. Some days I am more successful in my DM role than others.

As my husband often says, being a DM doesn't mean you have to be perfect, in fact, you can often be much more effective when you share your own fallible self openly with others. To be a truly effective DM you simply have to have a genuine passion for doing what you can to bring out the best in others.

The Designated Motivator: From Soup to Nuts

Kevin Brolin

For those of you who might be wondering—is Dawn Brolin's DM philosophy for real? Is motivating others and trying to bring people up to the level of greatness they are capable of really what she is all about? Is this what she really practices in her daily life? I can say, as someone who has lived with her for more than two decades, it's an emphatic, yes! Her dad was the same way. He is who she gets her DM gift from, honestly.

For some people who experience Dawn when she is going "full out" in her DM mode it may seem like she's a little "nuts" to use the colloquial expression for someone who is willing to do what she feels in her heart is the right thing—even if it makes her look silly or crazy.

As her husband and partner in life's journey, I know that Dawn's willingness to listen, to be present and to lift others up is encouraging and inspiring to everyone around her. It's one of the many attributes that made me "check the boxes" on my life partner list (yes, I had one!) when we first met.

Fast forward since those early days of dating and infatuation, and I can tell you, we have gone through the fire together. The most amazing and best thing is that we still like each other and love each other dearly.

Our marriage works on many fundamental levels and because we are both high achievers. She is the frontrunner in our family because she enjoys being "out there", but she also appreciates my own dedication to setting goals, accomplishing them and helping others do the same. It's something that I have done my whole life from my scouting days to my military career, while we raised our daughters and remained active in our church. While Dawn may be seen as bringing the "nuts" to the party—I take a simpler "soup" approach.

Let me explain this "soup to nuts" analogy more fully, because I have learned a lot from Dawn's approach to helping others and lifting them up whenever and wherever possible. I believe that in our "online video crazy" and social media-centric age, having people like Dawn creating real relationships is more important than ever. She is willing to go deep with people—in fact, she demands it of them and herself. She is willing to do anything and everything to have a DM impact as often as she can. It's her driving purpose.

However, I also believe that not everyone is going to be a DM in the same way. Instead of "nuts" some of us can bring a simple can of soup to the table—or to the food bank. You see, being a DM is not only about being "out there" like Dawn, and she doesn't believe that either.

Sometimes, for some of us, buying an extra can of soup at the store and donating it to a family in need can be as inspiring and motivating (or more so) as attending a motivational talk or reading a similar book. It's all about the DM mindset and how it moves and motivates you to take positive action in the life of another human.

Leadership has been an area of lifelong study for me—and I have often found in the many leadership classes and books I have studied that something is missing: the message that everybody has a gift and that no one's gift or accomplishment should be valued more than another person's. This is a fundamental truth that informs the DM philosophy.

Consider how our education system "rewards" only high achievers in academic endeavors. If you look beyond those grades and the people who can score high on test scores, which is amazing and very admirable, there's a whole array of other gifts and skills that need to be acknowledged and encouraged.

For example, my friend AJ can figure out how to fix a car in no time flat simply by putting hands on it—he's innately gifted in that area. Likewise, my pal Doug who is in the construction field can walk on a piece of land and intuitively envision how to build on it. Yet, our society often views these hands-on skills as "lesser than" those that require more academic training.

To me, being a DM is about helping others identify their greatness and find their own path and truth. As a DM, Dawn has made it a habit to help people get there—and that you should never feel "less than" because we are all worthy of recognition and celebration.

From a family perspective, the DM philosophy is definitely a positive in terms of showing our daughters the importance of lifting up others and maintaining an open and helpful heart. As Dawn has said in this book, there is a spectrum of DM "doing". She is definitely at the high end of it—which means, at times, she has sacrificed time with her own family to do for others. That sometimes comes with a price, both for our family unit and for her personally.

As a DM, Dawn definitely does a great job of listening, she is a cheerleader there is no doubt, but she doesn't always do all of the talking. Sometimes she "primes the pump" to allow the person she is engaging with to get what they need out of their system. She is very skilled at calling out self-defeating talk. She'll question if what someone is saying is really true to get them off the "but" trail and looking to see if they are actually speaking their truth.

She'll ask, "Is it true that you can't do these things?" Then she'll work with that person and get them to say, out of their own mouth, a different version of their truth. These are the moments when transformation happens.

Of course, like anyone else, Dawn as a DM needs to decompress. Her nickname in high school was Poke (after Gumby's sidekick) and that name has stuck to this day.

"I need Poke time," she will say. Always being sought after can be exhausting. Clients are reaching out, she gets referrals to do more, she gets requests to do more, her family and friends need her—and sometimes she just needs to be by herself.

When this happens, we are not offended, because we know that she'll come back recharged, refreshed and ready to take on the next DM challenge—which is exactly what the world needs her to do!

I also believe that we can all be DMs in a different way in our families and the other dimensions we are discussing here. I consider my husband, Kevin Brolin, one of the best examples of this "DM Spectrum," as he outlined in his narrative above.

I truly believe that the example of being a DM in your own home is one of the best life lessons you can offer to your children. However, depending on the degree to which you embrace it, there may also be sacrifices. No one can tell you more about this than my daughter, Emily. I believe she has an appreciation for the benefits of the DM philosophy which I have tried to impart on her as a mother and also some of the less desirable impact it has had on her due to my own approach, which is, of course, "all or nothing" as I have mentioned to before.

My Mom, The Designated Motivator: Sacrifice & Strength

Emily Brolin

"By watching my mom put her DM skills into action, I have seen the joy and fulfillment of helping others—and the sacrifice involved in balancing a career, personal goals and a family."

My mom and I are a lot alike—we look alike, we talk alike and we have the same extroverted personality. I have watched my mother go all in on helping others and it has been awesome to watch her do it all—have a career she loves, build a business to support our family and lend a helping hand, ear and voice whenever she can.

Both she and my father have taught me that you can never go wrong by helping someone. The level at which they offer kindness and assistance is amazing and rare.

As a very goal-oriented woman, my mom has provided my sister and I with an important role model. When you watch someone start from scratch and grow to become known nationwide is amazing. However, I have also seen that it comes with a price – there is sacrifice and she has had to become extremely strong and resilient. Not everyone will like you, she reminds us, and that's okay.

Another sacrifice has been time with her family. When she started building her business, my sibling and I were very small. She missed out on a lot of things because she was gone so much. We missed out on her, too.

That being said, I think her example has been extremely valuable for me. I can see her going after what makes her happy, fighting to be successful and not letting what others think stand in her way. I want to be an actress, which also takes a lot of work and dedication. I know, if she can pursue a dream others' might say isn't possible, so can I.

The way my mom raised us also made us independent. I know to get what you want; you have to hold your own. She inspired me with courage, too. I grew up in a small town and now live in a big city. At first it was very intimidating, but my mom was there for me.

"You just have to push yourself, be your own person and be successful," she encouraged me. She also told my sister and I that we can achieve and do anything—as long as we know and commit to the work it takes to get it.

I believe this is true. I also believe that the sacrifices and strength she has endured have allowed us to grow closer as a family. For myself, I understand why my mom has taken the path she has and I appreciate it.

I consider myself the "steady" in our family—although we are a lot alike, I also feel that I am able to pull back from my work and not get as wrapped up in my emotions. As I grow into an adult and pursue my career, I will keep in mind the importance of always keeping my family front and center, which is difficult to do when you have the passion to change the world like my mom does. .

All this being said, I could not have asked for two better role models as parents. My dad is also a steady force in our family—he is what I call my mom's "corkboard."

She gives him all of the details of what she's doing and what my sister and I need, then he actually makes sure it all gets done!

My parents truly have a partnership where they both share that fundamental value of being a DM, but they do it in different ways.

Thanks to both of them, as a college senior, I know my worth. This past year with COVID impacting the performing arts, it's been hard to maintain faith in my desire to be an actress. I know that my mom, dad and boyfriend have my back—they always do!

My mom gets me in ways no one else could and she is always there to encourage and to empower me when I need it. For example, a few years ago I was doing a show and I was just about ready to go on stage to do a beautiful solo when another girl said to me backstage, "You can't do it, don't even try."

I was freaking out and I called my mom who was sitting in the audience and I told her about it. She simply said, "Get your shit together, you are doing it!" She is definitely my best handler of the highest order.

It is a very rare and special relationship indeed.

A Family Legacy Built on the DM Philosophy

While it is admittedly difficult to hear some of the negative impacts of my DM drive (I believe every situation has its pros and cons), I do believe for the most part it has been a positive influence for our family. As Emily mentioned and you heard directly from my husband, Kevin, who also has the same foundational belief that we should encourage and lift others up whenever possible. As a couple, we just do it a little (okay, a lot) differently, which is exactly the point of this book and the tools I am sharing with you.

Make the DM philosophy your own—apply it through your actions and words in the ways that you feel are most effective for your family and the teams you are involved in. I believe that passing this legacy of helping others in the ways that you find most meaningful and being a DM to the level that you feel is beneficial for you is one of the most important gifts we can give our kids.

If you follow me on social media or have seen me speak, you might have heard me tell this story—for those of you who haven't, I simply like to call it "How My Children Saved My Business."

It's true that both of my daughters, deep down are DMs in their own rights. This is evidenced by how they actually stepped in to help me save my business just a few years ago when a sudden departure by a key employee during tax season threatened to take me down. It is because of our shared DM philosophy as a family (Kevin gets copious credit, too) that Emily and my other beautiful daughter, Kayla (who was born on my birthday!), were actually successful doing it!

Here's the quick 4-1-1 on the situation—you can also check out my talk about it from the Outbound 2017 event on YouTube.

As a CPA with an accounting and tax practice that serves several hundred businesses and their owners, you can imagine that the period from January through April each year can be pretty intense as my team and I prepare returns non-stop during that period. I depend on my team members to help me process these returns—I know that I cannot do it alone.

Then one day, a key team member, someone to whom I am very close, decided they wanted to leave my firm—smack dab in the middle of tax season. It was awful. I didn't know what I was going to do. I had all of these clients counting on me and I didn't have enough bandwidth from a CPA perspective to effectively review and file all of these returns on top of doing all of the other tasks required of me.

Just as I was wondering how on earth I was going to get everything done, my daughters (unprompted) in true DM spirit came into my bedroom—where, yes, I was having a bit of a momentary meltdown—and enthusiastically volunteered to help me out.

"We've watched you build this business, Mom," Kayla said, true to her sweet soul. "We're not going to let you lose it—not on our watch!"

Wow—talk about a proud mom moment! But more than the parental pride was a feeling that *it was* going to be *okay*. With the support and hard work of my DM daughters, we made it through that tax season. My business continued to flourish and I had the feeling that Kayla and Emily were going to carry the lessons we all learned well into adulthood.

Yes, the DM philosophy is definitely a family legacy that I live and love!

The Designated Motivator at Work

Next to my family unit, one of the most important places I find myself using my DM skills is in my business. So let me share one story that ties both of these DM dimensions together, so you can see how your DM influence in one area can create a ripple effect in others.

I firmly believe that even the most productive and successful people cannot accomplish their greatest achievements without some form of external motivation. The process of achieving a challenging goal is an experience that those of us in the business world are likely familiar with, especially when it comes to profitability, winning an award or simply accomplishing something great.

There is usually a driving force behind and around high-achieving people which keeps them striving to do whatever it takes to become a champion, to get a coveted award or to knock a project that they've been tasked with out of the park. They have someone who is motivating them or, they have an extraordinary ability to self-motivate at a very high level.

I see examples of this every day as a CPA and it's something I practice when working with my clients and motivating them to have successful businesses. I do it by helping them understand their numbers and encouraging them day-to-day or year-to-year, to manage their finances effectively.

If you are in business like me, you may be able to relate to the idea that practicing the DM philosophy is much more motivating in your work culture and for employees than other forms of authoritative, top-down management. This is backed up by research firm Gallup's recent study which showed companies with the highest engagement levels use recognition and praise as a powerful motivator. This is a stark contrast to using punishment and the removal of rewards or recognition.

In fact, Gallup found that employees who receive positive, individualized feedback on a regular basis (at least once a week) are more productive and receive higher loyalty and satisfaction scores from customers. They are also more likely to stay with their organization.

An example of the DM philosophy at work in my business comes from one of my favorite and most inspiring clients—Sheree, an entrepreneur and restaurant owner.

I help Sheree Goldstein by being a DM for her business and she takes on a DM role in her volunteer capacity in an organization that helps people with addictions get back on their feet. Consider her example below of the impact having a DM to help grow her business and how it can have a ripple effect in so many different areas, beyond just financial gain.

The Impact of a Designated Motivator in Business:

Sherree Goldstein Restaurant Owner, The Square Café and My Goodness Meals to Go

Dawn and I met at a women's entrepreneurial event called Spark & Hustle. Dawn asked me if I needed an accountant and at first I was hesitant because my accounting practice is very intricate. But she has expanded my view of what it means to manage my business—beyond just the financials.

She taught us we can flip eggs, be a true team and do the financials by looking at our business holistically. Dawn showed us how to engage with employees and build processes while forging a teamwork culture. She builds trust and it is very motivating to me as a business owner to keep doing more.

Dawn and I meet on FaceTime, which I wasn't used to before, but I like it now. We've become friends and she really is my Designated Motivator. I feel what she does for me in her capacity as my CPA is similar to my work at the rehab center, where I volunteer. She brings the power of teamwork, trust and motivation to my business.

It's amazing to see people changing their realization of who they are and growing in to their potential in this way. Like Dawn does for me with my business, the people I work with at the rehab center start looking at their lives from a different angle and it changes everything.

This is really what Dawn has done for our business. She has given us a different angle and helped us to pay attention to the bigger picture. This view is super important and she has provided us with the motivation to look at our business with different knowledge so we can make better decisions and grown the future.

Your DM Mindset, Business and the Challenges of Being Human

I work hard every day to not take it personally when someone calls my office and gets all up in my grill. You know *that* person, when you see the caller ID and your brain immediately says, "Here we go!"

I have found, if you take a step back and think about it, a person's actions and communication may not be about you. You have no idea what has happened to that person in the last five minutes, five hours, or five days. Maybe they have a horrible home life or a wild child who is just wearing them out. Or maybe they made a poor business decision that they don't know how to recover from. You have absolutely no idea, so who the heck are you to judge them without the facts?

Obviously, in the professional and personal paradigms of life, we are not meant to be punching bags. However, having the ability to be sympathetic, listen and acknowledge where you and the person you are dealing with are, in that moment, can be transformative for both parties.

You will always have those people who, no matter what you say or do, will be assholes. You can't help everyone, but you can try!

You never know when a negative experience will change how you proceed tomorrow. We all have these experiences, but few of us take action on them. As a DM, you need to ask yourself how you can take positive and productive action in the moment as you deal with challenging situations at work and with people who, like all of us, are dealing with the challenges of being human during our business interactions.

The Designated Motivator in the Classroom: Bigger, Brighter Futures

I recently started teaching as an adjunct professor in the accounting department at Eastern Connecticut State University. As you can imagine, this role is for me, a little bit of DM heaven.

When I enter the classroom as a teacher, I approach each day thinking about how I can help these students do their best both with the coursework and with their future career planning. Since I'm working specifically in the accounting department, I am using the opportunity to encourage kids that they can go out on their own and run their own accounting firm. They can do anything they want in the accounting profession.

I want students to think and move beyond what is typically "sold" as the path to success in this profession. It's not just go work for the big four and be a person who works 80 hours a week, in a situation where you're basically owned by that company.

As a DM it's my job and passion to let them know that there's more out there that they can do. I also encourage them to find *their* passion within accounting, I know that for those of you who don't "do the numbers" this may sound ridiculous, but it isn't. It's an actual real thing. Christian, one of my students, provides the perfect example of this.

Christian is one of my current students at Eastern Connecticut State University. Using my DM skills, I was able to get to know him on a different level, much deeper than just lecturing to him as part of a group of students. I got to know Christian, particularly what motivated him and what his concerns and goals were. It turns out that he wasn't so sure that the typical accounting path was the right one for him.

As you can imagine, he found this worrisome, especially when he has spent a significant amount of time and money pursuing his accounting degree. What he needed was a new vision of how he could utilize his skills to make a bigger impact on the world. A new way of approaching a career in accounting.

I shared with him my training as a Certified Fraud Examiner and my work in this area—yep, I am an accounting cop! This opened a whole new world to him and he researched potential career paths available with this kind of training. He decided that he would like to pursue a career with the FBI, investigating accounting fraud and serving our country at the same time!

This is another example of how your DM superpower really can create change in the world. Imagine if I had not reached out to Christian—he might have become so demoralized with his career choice that he went into another academic program, or resigned himself to having a career he did not enjoy. What a waste of talent and passion. Not on my watch! And I hope you also see the value of not letting it happen on your watch either!

What are your Key DM Dimensions?

There you have it. A little bit of insight into my key DM Dimensions. Now I want you to think about what yours are, and how you can use the next few chapters that detail the Designated Motivator Toolkit to maximize your impact in these areas.

I truly believe that a Designated Motivator can do absolutely anything in absolutely any part of their life if they put their mind to it. It isn't just about sports. It's about people, and it's about how you can positively impact another person on a level that lights them up and moves them to action. This is what the rest of this book is about: YOU taking action to move from having a pivotal experience, to using it to help and lift up others, so they can do the same.

The bigger goal is for all of us to create a #MotivationMovement which makes our world better by helping in small and big ways to encourage people so they are happier, more productive and ultimately, can utilize the full power of the potential and passion within themselves.

The Designated Motivator Toolkit

As a DM, you probably already instinctively know that when you positively impact another person, you bring yourself--and them--up to another level. It's a level that if everyone embraced it in some capacity, and became a designated motivator, we could literally change the world. And I really believe that. That's not just pen on paper. That's passion and it's true and it's a fact. It's not a theory, it's not a concept. It actually works. Try it yourself, you might just be surprised.

Help Us Start The #MotivationMovement

I wrote this book because I truly believe that we need a #MotivationMovement across this country and really, the world! There is far too much potential wasted due to lack of engagement and encouragement in business and our personal lives. Imagine what just a little encouragement and empowerment could do for you--and the people around you. It truly can make a life-changing difference on so many levels driving your personal beliefs, achievement and business goals forward, past all limitations!

I understand that even if you are the "head" of one of the "teams" mentioned above, you may feel like you are not quite up to being the DM. That's fair, not everyone needs to be out front as the leader *and* the DM. However, I do think it is important to know where you stand in this regard so you can either delegate the DM duties to someone else, or evolve your own DM capabilities to become a UDM (Ultimate

Designated Motivator) who truly can take your team and its individual members to the next level.

This is why it is important to understand not only how to be motivated but what drives that motivation in each of us. We're all different but according to renowned psychologist and researcher, David McClelland, who developed a fundamental theory of motivation, there are three drivers of motivation common to all of us: a need for achievement, a need for affiliation and a need for power.

Also, we all differ in what our dominant motivator is, which, McClelland says, we learn through our experiences and the culture we are immersed in.

So which of these drivers is the primary one that defines what I call, your Motivational Mindset? The quiz below can help you determine what your primary motivator is. Once you know that, we'll dive a little deeper into each of these three motivational drivers so you can recognize and leverage them in others as a DM.

So go ahead, take the quiz (I know I am a sucker for these self-assessment tools, too!) and I'll meet you after your self-analysis in the next chapter with some tools to help you take your new found Motivator Mindset to the next level so you can start applying it to fulfill your role as a Designated Motivator.

Your Motivational Mindset Self-Assessment Quiz

Which of the three motivational drivers shapes your Motivational Mindset? Answer the following questions and keep track of how many A, B and C answers you select! You know how this works...whichever letter you have the most of in your answers, corresponds with the Motivational Mindset questions below.

For each set of questions, choose the answer that you feel describes you best:

Motivation Mindset 1

A. I have a strong need to set and accomplish challenging goals.
B. I feel good when my achievements are recognized by others.
C. I like knowing what is going to happen when.

Motivation Mindset 2

A. Taking calculated risks is appealing to me.
B. If there is an award or prize I want to win it!
C. I like working in a group.

Motivation Mindset 3

A. I invite feedback on my progress and achievements.
B. Friendly competition is a wonderful thing.
C. I prefer to collaborate than to compete.

Motivation Mindset 4

A. I like to work alone.
B. People tell me I am good at making my point clear.
C. Being part of a team is appealing to me.

Motivation Mindset 5

A. I never met a task list I didn't love.
B. I love making new connections and learning about people.
C. I try to keep the peace in my relationships for the most part.

If you answered mostly As:

You are an Achievement Club Member

You enjoy challenges and thrive on overcoming difficult problems or situations, making achievement your primary motivational driver. Another clue: you do your best work either alone or with other high achievers. If you belong to The Achievement Club, you likely also value feedback on your progress so you can use it to improve and are known for giving your own brand of fair and balanced reviews.

If you scored mostly Bs:

You are an Active Affiliate

Are you someone who enjoys group work but who doesn't like uncertainty and risk? Do you tend to take things personally? Then you are motivated primarily with the need to be affiliated with other people and to be part of something like a team or an organization that you believe in. Unlike the other two Motivational Mindsets detailed here, people who are affiliate-driven in their Motivation Mindset often don't want to stand out. If this resonates with you, then you may be someone who can be a very effective Designated Motivator to lift up others.

If you scored mostly Cs:

You are a Power Broker

Do you want to be in charge and do your best work that way? If you also like to compete and take on goal-oriented projects or tasks then power is likely your primary motivation. Another clue? You may also be a very effective negotiator, especially in situations where you need to sell your ideas or the reasons behind wanting to reach a goal.

Now you know what the primary driver is behind your Motivation Mindset, you will be able to recognize the same or a different driver in others. This is the magic key that many people who have the gift of being able to move others to action and the desire to do so come by naturally. So let's look at how you can leverage this new knowledge as you master the key skills you need to be an effective DM.

Mastering the
Designated Motivator Skill Set

I totally understand that the ability to self-motivate and to motivate others doesn't come easily to everyone. Even those who are naturally inclined and inspired to be the DM in a given situation may need some extra help every now and then to maintain their focus and direct their energy effectively.

I have been asked a lot about how I know what to do to be a DM. The truth is, there isn't a DM playbook per se, I have just honed the skill set I am sharing with you below over time.

These are the practices that have consistently worked for me and the people for whom I have been a DM and those who have been a DM for me. You might have other skills that you want to incorporate in your own DM approach. Feel free to share them on social media using the #MotivationMovement hashtag, too!

1. **Be observant to see where you are needed.** One of the key skills of any DM is the ability to observe people in various situations and pick up on clues that an individual may need some assistance from you. Here are some examples of signs people may need a DM intervention. You may need to step in if you see someone who:

- Isn't performing at the level that you know they are capable of.

- Is routinely negative and disengaged from their work or their primary functions.

- Uses self-deprecating words and seems preoccupied with problems.

- Is having a hard time coping with external stressors and is feeling anxious or overwhelmed because of them.

- Seems to be frequently up and down in their mood.

An example of this type of observation that I can offer is through my coaching with the Lady Warriors team. One of the players, Julia, has the cutest dimples ever. When she was smiling and happy she had a whole bunch of dimples. I knew she was in need of a DM boost when those dimples were not present!

Another point here: if you see something, say something. Even if you have to approach it gently, and remember, if someone is truly in distress, it's time to move from being a DM to being a responsible party to get them professional help with a potentially urgent mental health situation.

2. **Invest time in learning about others.** In today's fast-paced, crazy-busy world it is important as a DM (and a good human) to connect with other people on a deeper level. This is important not only to try to help and motivate them, but also for your own well-being. Humans need meaningful connections with other humans.

Everyone has some issue or area of life that they struggle with. This might be a short-term problem or a chronic condition. As a DM when you invest time to get to know someone beyond a superficial level, you will find areas where you can offer support, encouragement and motivation to help someone get through these issues.

For example, during my softball coaching, I make a conscious effort to get to know each of the kids individually. On the 2019 Lady Warriors team, I knew that one player liked candy for a snack, and another player's mom was giving her a hard time. I learned by spending time listening and observing the team members that some of the girls struggled to keep their grades up. Others had boyfriend problems or suffered from anxiety. It turns out, there was an awful lot going on under the surface with these players.

The same is true for many of the other people I meet on a regular basis—and I am sure you see the same thing in your world, too.

Bottom line: we all have stress, fear, anxiety and other feelings or beliefs that can diminish our capacity to feel we are worthy, capable or motivated to reach our goals. As a DM, I invested the time to understand where team members were coming from on a personal level so that I could intervene as appropriate.

3. **Understand what makes people tick.** Applying the DM principles is not a one-size-fits-all endeavor. You need to learn what motivates others on an individual level. Using the three main types of motivators from the DM Mindset section—Achievement, Affiliation, or Power—is a great start.

Then figure out what it is that makes *your* particular Motivatee tick. If the person you are working with a member of the Achievement Club, learn what they're passionate about. How can you help them set goals which align with their aspirations and interests, then give them the tools to achieve them?

> **1. Use eye contact and body language.** It goes without saying that as a DM, you must respect all rules and social norms when answering your calling to help others in the ways that I am outlining here. In today's culture and social environment, a hands-off approach is often encouraged and established boundaries must be respected.

However, there are little ways that you can use physical cues and body language to both understand your Motivatee and also offer the comfort, compassion and non-verbal communication that so many of us need.

Eye contact, standing or sitting comfortably close to whom you are talking to, offering a compassionate hand to hold—and if appropriate and welcomed— a hug can all do wonders to ease anxiety, allow people to know that you really are open and ready to receive what they have to say and that you truly care.

Don't underestimate the power of your physical presence and body language to help you forge a meaningful connection with those people around you who are waiting for someone to inspire, encourage and lift them up.

2. **Vary your motivation techniques.** Using different forms of motivation, depending on the situation, is very important. Sometimes the crazy antics and humor work really well, but sometimes a listening ear and a hug is what is in order.

You may be surprised how powerful your DM impact can be by simply listening in a non-judgmental way to how someone is feeling and what is going on in their life. You need to gauge these situations. In some, you may need to push back on what you are hearing to help the person who is struggling see a different truth about their situation. Or in others, take a gentler approach using your empathetic skills.

3. **Create positive interactions.** The key takeaway for any DM interaction you have with another human is to have the goal of leaving them better than you found them. I try to practice this as much as possible as I go through life. I will admit, some days and some moments I do better than others, but on the whole, I try to practice the DM philosophy whenever I interact with someone.

If you aren't a person who wants to go "all in" on being a DM in a formal sense for a team, work, school or family situation. Then I encourage you to at least try to brighten and lighten someone's day when you are grocery shopping or interacting with a service provider. This may seem like a small thing, but it can have a big impact!

I recently stopped at my local dollar store to pick up snacks for the softball team (I find food can be a very powerful motivating force in many cases.) and as I was checking out with my cart full of goodies at 8 a.m. in the morning, I joked with the cashier not to judge me—these snacks weren't all for me! I could see her mood lighten instantly and she bantered back and forth with me as she rang up my order.

"You're so nice!" the cashier said and I could tell she meant it. I imagine that as she goes through her routine on most days she will get a few nice people who come through her line and probably some more challenging customers too. I just hope that I made her day a little better and that the positive interaction sustains her in some way through the less enjoyable parts of her job. Better yet, I hope she may even pass it along to her co-workers and customers!

As you can see from this example, you have the power to create a DM domino effect in small, simple, but significant ways!

> 4. **Help others see a brighter future.** As a DM, it is important to keep creating a vision of the future for those you are working with—this is especially true in a team setting. Whether it is an employee, a client, an athlete, or a family member you'll want to help them see a new way of handling a tough situation or advancing their skills to accomplish more in the future.

In addition to helping them develop a new and more positive mindset, you can also help them develop new skills that they can use to make better choices or try new things by playing to their strengths, interests and capabilities. This will help them keep "facing forward" and moving toward their goals.

5. **Provide positive and productive feedback.** While I am certainly all about keeping things light and making people feel good as a DM I also know that to truly transform people sometimes you have to get real about a situation. This is especially true if the person you are a DM for is practicing self-sabotaging behavior. A key skill for most DMs is being able to provide personalized, positive and productive feedback to others on their progress.

One way to do this is the "Feedback Sandwich" approach (See, I told you I think food is a real motivator—whether it is real or not!). Start with something positive, then provide some insight on an issue that is not being handled well, then end with a positive about how you believe in the person's ability to overcome the challenge or make changes in their behavior.

6. **Pile on the praise and compliments.** Building and nurturing real relationships with others requires that you can have real conversations with people. It also requires that you can give compliments and praise freely when they are deserved—so strengthen your DM skill set by practicing positive words on a daily basis.

This may sound simple, but so many of us go through our days not showing any form of appreciation, gratitude or positive praise for all of the things others do. As a DM make it a habit not to take anything in your life for granted, from a family member finally remembering to close the refrigerator door (Nice work keeping those veggies fresh!) to piling on praise for someone who just accomplished something major at work, let your positive comments flow freely as often as you can.

Soon you'll be acknowledging praiseworthy acts without thinking about it and you may just have a DM ripple effect that benefits everyone around you!

7. Expand your network of encouragement experts.
Building on the last point above, as a DM, one of the key ways you can have maximum impact is to bring other people into your network of encouragement experts—so they can help to reinforce and reiterate your own efforts with an individual or a team.

Of course, be judicious about confidentiality when it comes to personal situations that you may be helping people with, but in most cases, encouraging people all around you to lift up others is something that they can get excited about.

In other words, let others in on your DM superpower secret—and their own—so that together you can all work to be an encouraging source of power for as many people as possible.

Now Put Your DM Skills Into Action

Technically, right now I am talking to the natural-born motivators. You know who you are. For those of you who don't necessarily think of themselves as DMs, I'll get to you soon, too. You won't be left out! The point being, after the experience of coaching the Lady Warrior team, I realized that no matter what I do in life, no matter what situation I am in, that I have the ability to be a powerful motivator.

In fact, I believe that most of us have the ability to leave people better than we found them. With this in mind, there is something very important that I want to draw your attention to: **Having a pivotal experience and doing something with it are two totally different actions.**

Once you have an experience such as mine with coaching the softball team, you are then (in my very strong opinion) required to do something with it. The obvious thing to do from my perspective is to use what you have learned to help others. For me, helping meant asking, "How can you motivate people in your business, in your personal life and in your friendships?"

I began to believe (and make the decision in my brain) that it was time to start kicking some ass as a DM and taking names. And in that I mean it was time for me to **DO SOMETHING**! Seriously, if you have an experience you consider pivotal in your life, do something with it that will cause change around you.

Make a choice to leave your comfort zone and create your own #MotivationMovement!

Most of us have listened to podcasts, attended a webinar, attended a motivational talk and then *done nothing with it*. You may have enjoyed that experience, that talk and that feeling of motivation while you were in the moment but then you didn't take it to the next level. I urge you to make a difference now. Choose to leave your comfort zone and make a difference for yourself, your family, your business or workplace—anywhere and everywhere that you can!

Part of the reason why I believe it is difficult to act on those experiences is that we tend to come out of that moment and quickly move back into our comfortable routine of our thought patterns and schedule. We typically move right back into the same habits we have always had. Instead, I challenge you with this:

What **MUST** happen at this point is that a decision needs to be made by **YOU**.

You (and only you) can take that experience and decide that you aren't going to do the same thing over and over again.

You must make the decision that you will not follow the pattern of insanity and do the same thing while expecting different results.

The critical step that needs to be taken, the one thing that will change the course and path of your life and the lives of others, **is to move your ass and get shit done!** You have to be a doer, not a talker. Don't waste another book, another webinar, another conference, another game, another motivational talk. In the immortal words of Nike, "Just do it!" and do something with your experience.

Not An End...But the Beginning of Something Phenomenal

"Do it no matter what. If you believe in it, it is something very honorable. If somebody around you or your family does not understand it, then that's their problem. But if you do have a passion, an honest passion, just do it." — Mario Andretti

Here's what I want you to do after you read this book: Start your own #MotivationMovement.

DO SOMETHING!

Consider the experiences you have had and how you can use them to help others. How can you help other people? How can you encourage them? Be their cheerleaders? Make sure they understand and value their worth?

This is not a book that is meant to stay on a shelf. Pass it along to the next DM, highlight it, revisit the DM Toolkit and make your own notes. Embrace your inner DM and make things happen!

This is what I intend to do! I want to make things happen, too!

I am still close with many of the kids from our 2019 team. I'm still coaching, too. Of course, 2020 was a terrible year with COVID impacting so many people—including our players. We lost five players who graduated, the rest of the team came back. We were on track to win the National Tournament in 2020. Then COVID stripped that opportunity away from those kids. A tough lesson in the fact that life isn't fair. However, I am still thankful that they at least had the experience in 2019 to go to the National Tournament, something they will never, ever forget. And neither will I. This is where the magic and the real superpower of being a DM comes into play for me once again. It's in the action of creating long-term impact on someone else's self-image and level of self-motivation by believing in them, creating positive experiences for them and forging deep relationships that leave a lasting impression. If we are lucky, as DM's we can start a #MotivationMovement that also leaves a legacy for those who come next.

As I am wrapping up this book, we are now in the spring season of 2021. Something amazing is brewing with this group of young women. As of this last passing of my pen (well, keyboard), the team has embraced the #MotivationMovement and is currently 20-0 and ranked third in the country. I truly believe that these young women are being each others, DM every single day. They encourage, lift up , and embrace each moment they have together with everything in their souls. And the end result, I am certain, will be everything they have dreamed of and everything they have worked for. The movement is happening with them and I cannot wait to see what they can achieve together!

As you may have guessed, or maybe experienced by now, I am a talker but more importantly a doer—there is no doubt. It's part of my unique DM approach—I am who I am, man! However, I believe that creating a safe space for others to find their voices is one of the highest and best skills you can hone as a DM. To this end, I want to close this book with someone else's words. They are the words of Kamdynn Moroney, one of our 2019 team members.

Like so many people you meet, Kamdynn needed a DM, and I was honored to have the chance to get to know her as her assistant coach and offer her the support and encouragement she needed to realize her own sensational self, her amazing skills and the strength to surmount her story. She did all the work, as her DM, I just gave her the space and guidance to do it.

A DM to Depend On: Kamdynn's Story

Personally, Dawn has been my Designated Motivator. She believes in me and cares about me. She made me see that I could accomplish more than what I thought I could.

When I first met Dawn, like many of my teammates, we really thought she was crazy and wondered who she really was, but, truth be told, we all immediately liked her. She has a way of connecting with people which was comforting and engaging. We felt like we now had someone that we felt comfortable opening up to and helping us through issues we had on and off the field.

No matter what is going on. Dawn's goal was to convince us that we had potential we didn't even realize. She believed in us from day one and spent the rest of the season shoving that into our brains. Because of that, we were able to place third in the country in a season that we thought would be just like all the others. Her passion for our belief in ourselves made us want to be better players and be the absolute best team we could be.

From a team perspective, while we were all good players, we just didn't play cohesively in past years. Dawn convinced us that we were extremely talented and had the ability to go as far as we wanted in the three tournaments we competed in that year.

Going to college was a big adjustment for me. Many people tried to help me. I just didn't feel comfortable opening up to anyone about the challenging events that I had experienced in my life. Dawn took the time to understand those challenges and simply said, she just cared enough to try to understand what I was going through.

Dawn empathized with me—she didn't just tell me that I was going to be okay. She knew that my struggles were real, and that I just needed someone to actually care about me enough to listen. She was able to see my potential and was committed 100% to consistently check in on me and help me when I needed it the most. She knew that I had my own passion for helping other people. She made me believe that I could become a social worker, get my master's degree and use my experience to help others.

Our relationship grows every day. I go to her for everything. She always wants to help. She really doesn't care what it takes to support me.

Dawn has been my Designated Motivator. She believes in me and cares about me. She made me see that I had more to give than what I thought I did. She helped me see that even though I struggle with life sometimes, what I need to do is envision a brighter, better path forward. I cannot think of any better motivation than that as I work toward achieving my goals and dreams. I definitely intend to be a DM for as many people as possible in the future. There is so much more I could say, but I am just thankful she is in my life for good.

YOU ROCK!

WELCOME TO THE TEAM!

Make It Official

Get Your Exclusive DM Bonuses at DawnBrolin.com

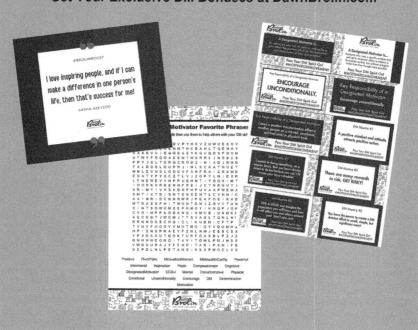

The Designated Motivator name and concept is the exclusive intellectual property of Dawn. W. Brolin. No part of this book or associated properties may be reprinted electronically or in print without express permission of the author.

What People Are Saying About
The Designated Motivator

"As you start to read this book, you will feel the energy yourself. You will feel a shift inside you that can never be undone. You will find that there is a Designated Motivator waiting to be awakened in you and anyone you, well, designate.

When you become a DM it exponentially improves every area of your life. Your business will improve, your personal life will improve, the people in your orbit will be more engaged. You will thrive. The people who benefit from the DM will also have improvement throughout their lives."

- Mike Michalowicz, Author, *Profit First* and Designated Motivator for Entrepreneurs

"Many of us are thrust into leadership not knowing what that exactly means. We struggle to do it well. We try hard and yet we are not sure if we are having an impact. The best leaders are DMs, what Dawn calls a Designated Motivator. DMs have influence to positively change behavior and that is what leadership is at its core. This book is refreshing in that it reminds us that all of us can be a DM to our peers, our colleagues and our communities. As you read it, you recall those who have been important DMs in your own life, and that makes you smile. That feeling reminds you why and inspires you to go out into the world today and be a great leader one DM moment at a time."

- Jody Padar, The Radical CPA, Author & Strategic Leader

"Most of the time when I read a business book, I feel like the author is talk "at" me and telling me all of the things that they know how to do better and that is why they are writing to book to shout from the mountaintop of their superiority and their ability to share it with us out of the kindness of their heart.

Dawn Brolin is not like that, in fact Dawn is the person that I can genuinely say is like no other person on this planet, but I knew that before I read her book. Throughout the whole book, Dawn is talking to us and never at us. It is almost like she is in our head because before we can ask her a question about what she is talking about, she writes in a way that she is already responding to the questions that she knows that we will have, it really is like having a conversation with her. She not only talks about but gives us real live relatable examples of when things worked and when they did not, as we all know that we can sometimes learn more from our failures and Dawn is not afraid to put those out there but embraces them.

The meaning of "WIN", will change my mindset forever now, it is not the being on top but "What's Important Now?"

Dawn practices what she preaches and now I have a name that I can put to her actions, she is a true leader. I would recommend this book not to just business owners but to anyone that is looking to find their place, at home, at work, in hobbies; this knowledge share is good for any age or education level, it is not your normal business book."

- Robin Hall
President & Principal Consultant
VARC Solutions

My DM Action Plan Notes

Use this space to take note, jot down ideas and plan your own #MotivationMovement!

Made in the USA
Middletown, DE
18 August 2022

71615562R00056